Training Your Parrot

Title page: Siegfried ready for school.

ISBN 0-87666-872-4

Distributed in the UNITED STATES by T.F.H. Publications, Inc., 211 West Sylvania Avenue, Neptune City, NJ 07753; in CANADA by Rolf C. Hagen Ltd., 3225 Sartelon Street, Montreal 382 Quebec; in ENGLAND by T.F.H. (Great Britain) Ltd., 11 Ormside Way, Holmethorpe Industrial Estate, Redhill, Surrey RH1 2PX; in AUSTRALIA AND THE SOUTH PACIFIC by Pet Imports Pty. Ltd., Box 149 Brookvale 2100 N.S.W., Australia; in SOUTH AFRICA by Multipet (Pty.) Ltd., 30 Turners Avenue, Durban 4001. Published by T.F.H. Publications Inc. Ltd., The British Crown Colony of Hong Kong.

Training Your Parrot
THE EDUCATION OF SIEGFRIED

KEVIN MURPHY

One of Siegfried's favorite games is flying from his play stand to his trainer's hand for a treat.

Opposite:
The effects of good pet care are seen in Siegfried's good body weight and fine plumage.

Photography
Jerry Allen: 68.
William Allen: 134, 135, 153.
Glen Axelrod: 102, 103.
Dr. H.R. Axelrod: 23, 26 top, 40, 107, 138.
Tony Caravaglia: 14, 15, 98, 162.
Kerry Donnelly: 80.
Ray Hanson: 26 bottom, 110, 111, 114, 115, 118, 119, 122, 123, 179.
Max Mills: front and back endpapers, title page, 6, 7, 10, 11, 12, 18, 19, 20, 30, 32, 34, 44, 46, 47, 48, 49, 50, 51, 52, 58, 59, 66, 67, 70, 74, 75, 78, 79, 82, 83, 84, 86, 87, 88, 89, 90, 91, 92, 94, 95, 96, 109, 112, 120, 125, 126, 127, 129, 131, 136, 139, 145, 148, 155, 158, 160, 163, 166, 167, 170, 171, 174, 175, 178, 182, 183, 186, 187.
A.J. Mobbs: 31 top.
Dr. J. Moore: 22 top.
Dr. E.J. Mulawka: 71, 99.
Kevin and Ellie Murphy: 28, 151, 172, 176, 184, 188.
Vince Serbin: 27, 31 bottom, 104, 106.
Louise Van der Meid: 36, 37.

Contents

The ruffling of Siegfried's neck and head feathers always signifies that he is about to vocalize. Here he sings a song with the author.

Opposite:
Vocalizing with the author isn't confined to speech. Siegfried also enjoys human-style whistling and shows his skill by providing instant replays of whistled sounds and musical phrases.

The author with his prize pupil, Siegfried.

Introduction

Much of the information about parrots available to us is provided by two sources: ornithologists supply scholarly, scientific data obtained from studies of the birds in their natural habitat, and aviculturists provide equally valuable information based on the study of birds in captivity. Experts of both groups rely on each other to some extent in the exchange of information as specific needs arise. As aviculturists are experts in the breeding of birds in captivity and in the many complex aspects of successfully maintaining the various species, their experience is of particular interest to the pet owner. Let me enlarge on this a bit by stating that aviculturists cater more to the hobby aspect of birds than do the ornithologists.

This writer claims to be neither ornithologist nor aviculturist; my level of involvement and expertise fits neither category. As a pet owner with a keen interest in parrots, I observed that there was a need for information generated by a third source: pet owners themselves. Many have considerable knowledge and experience which they generally do not make available to others.

The prospective pet-parrot owner should understand that most of what is known about keeping birds as pets comes not as the result of serious scientific inquiry but as the result of collected individual experiences. Many of these experiences are far from typical because many unusual birds and unusual people are brought together into relationships which result in an amazing development of abilities.

The African Grey Parrot is highly regarded for its talking ability and for its reputation as a gentle pet.

Opposite:
The Mexican Double Yellow-head is considered to be one of the most talented of the Amazon parrots. Siegfried shows the alertness and curiosity which is typical of Amazons.

There are many stories about the enthusiast who reads all the books, buys a parrot, and, although he follows all the "rules" faithfully, can't get the bird to do anything except eat and mess up its cage. There are just as many stories about the nonenthusiast who visits a friend who owns a vicious, nontalking parrot. The visitor says hello to the bird; the bird repeats the hello and almost falls off his perch in his eagerness to make friends.

Each bird is a unique individual with its own complex array of quirks and characteristics which will determine its potential as a pet. It must also be said that each of us humans has his own complex array of talents, with all their diversities. Very often, but not always, the personalities of a human and a parrot converge into one of those friendships which illustrates the kinship that can develop between man and his fellow creatures.

You will undoubtedly read other books about parrots besides this one, and I hope you will keep in mind that each author is offering personal experiences in the *art* of training and taming parrots. There is very little if any true science available on the subject. Your own experience with a parrot will in many respects be unique because both you and the bird are unique individuals.

There are no guarantees about what any one bird and its owner can accomplish together. Your pet parrot may become tame immediately, or it may take months. The bird may demonstrate very early a desire and talent for speech, or it may never happen.

It is my purpose in this volume to provide you, the reader, with such information as you may need to help you decide on whether or not you want to own a parrot, what kind, and how it should be cared for, tamed, and trained. I have taken the approach of writing about one specific bird, a Mexican Double Yellow-headed Amazon named Siegfried. Unavoidably this approach becomes somewhat biographical, but I believe this has the positive effect of being able to recount specific incidents in training and the effects they produced. This is far preferable for the prospective pet owner than to explain a principle of training and then to leave him wondering if it has ever been found to be valid. In the course of studying parrots I have sought out the published works of ornithologists and aviculturists. It has also been very interesting and informative to discuss the subject with many pet-store owners, a bird tamer, and a number of individual bird owners.

Coupled with my own enjoyable observations of Siegfried I hope to offer you a well-balanced narrative of personal experiences and some ornithological and some avicultural information. Above all, I hope to provide a practical guide to assist you in your enjoyment of owning a parrot.

Kevin Murphy

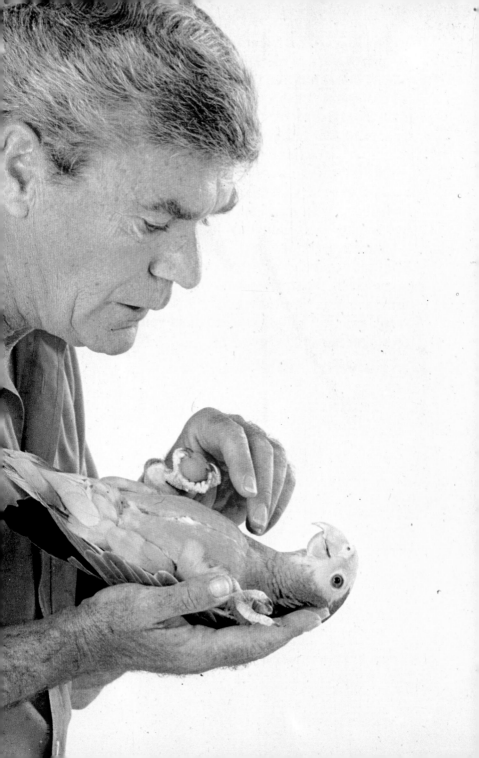

Siegfried often pauses during play and training sessions to attend to his plumage.

Opposite:
The tamer the bird, the greater the degree of trust in the trainer. Here, Siegfried confidently assumes an unnatural position for a bird—lying on his back in his trainer's hand.

19

Most parrots have a predilection for chewing, and Siegfried is no exception.

The Pet Parrot in Your Home

Many readers of this volume have not yet become owners of parrots. I suspect that in many cases the purchase of the book was made in order to learn something about the subject before making the decision to buy a bird. This chapter is intended to answer some of the most pertinent questions which I feel will be uppermost in the minds of prospective owners. The common image of a parrot which most people have is that of a gaudily colored bird, which can be taught to perform clever tricks, makes witty remarks, and in many films sits on the shoulder of a one-legged pirate. In fact, parrots fit that description very easily, yet it is far too restrictive a description, considering the vast number of parrots in all shapes and sizes which are available.

The scientific name for the *order* of birds to which all parrots belong is *Psittaciformes*. Within the order birds are grouped into *families* (cockatoos, lories, and parrots) and *subfamilies*. These groups are further divided (more or less according to *genus*) into macaws, Amazons, conures, lovebirds, grass parakeets, parrotlets, etc.

The first consideration for the reader, then, is what parrot would be right for you. The choices range from the common, inexpensive budgies which make excellent pets to the largest of all parrots, the giant macaws, whose size places some limitations on their suitability for most homes. In between are many other species

Lovebirds, which average about five inches in length, are small parrots. After they have been tamed, like this Peach-faced Lovebird, they can be trained to do tricks and may even learn to imitate a few words.

Opposite:
Above: The macaws include some of the largest members of the parrot family—the Hyacinth Macaw is about thirty-four inches in length. Macaws are generally known more for their ability to learn tricks than for their ability to mimic speech. *Below:* Cockatiels are medium-sized parrots about twelve inches long. Popular because they make friendly and affectionate pets, they can learn to talk reasonably well and are commonly available.

commonly chosen as pets. Cockatiels are highly regarded as affectionate pets, and lovebirds are readily available and inexpensive. Among the larger birds are many species and subspecies of cockatoos and parrots which are popular because of their reputations as good pets and for their talking ability.

The author's own introduction to birds as pets came about in a rather unusual way. One beautiful sunny morning I was sitting reading and was disturbed by a strange chattering sound. As I looked up, one of our cats trotted in from the patio holding a Budgerigar in her mouth. After closing the door to prevent the cat from leaving, I was able to rescue the bird. Fortunately the bird was completely unhurt, although it was naturally very annoyed at such treatment. This incident—and failure to find a neighbor who had lost the budgie—started me off on a study of all the fascinating aspects of pet birds.

Each kind of bird, of course, has its own particular qualities as a pet and requirements for care. In making your selection some thought must be given to what commitment of time you want to devote to your parrot. Kelly, our little Budgerigar, is typical of budgies in that it makes very little demand for care and attention as compared to Siegfried, a typical Amazon, who gets about three hours a day of playing, taming, and training.

The kind of relationship you can enjoy with a parrot really depends largely on yourself. All kinds of parrots have a good intelligence level and enjoy human friendship, although some species exhibit these qualities more than others. Experienced bird owners have preferences for their favorite birds; therefore I will avoid making comparisons and suggesting that one kind of bird is more desirable than another.

I have found that Amazon parrots can provide a level of companionship and interaction at least comparable to that of a faithful dog. An Amazon is superior to the dog in one obvious respect, vocal communication, but you'll probably have to get your pipe and slippers yourself. It possesses a broad array of natural chuckles, clucks, whistles, and groans, plus its ability to mimic its owner. Amazon owners have a tendency to believe these parrots are the ultimate pets.

Certain groups of parrots, including Amazons, have rather bad reputations for the amount of noise they make. You should take this into consideration when you're deciding the kind of bird you want. Yet an individual of any species may be atypical of its fellows—noisier or quieter—so the best you can do is attempt to find the individual bird with which you can be most compatible. A noisy Amazon makes an irritatingly loud, sharp natural call which I would equate roughly with the loud, high-pitched barking of a medium-sized dog. In the chapter on speech training I mention that with training and attention you can exercise some control over an Amazon's call.

The prospective parrot owner should not be overly concerned about the bird being either a smelly or messy pet, provided that recommendations for daily cage maintenance are followed. Even the largest Amazons cannot possibly make enough mess in the cage in one day to earn a reputation for being messy birds. Unfortunately, some bird owners become a bit lax in their housekeeping, and the bird gets the blame.

Feeding, as mentioned in the chapter on daily care, is complex for the larger birds. If you do decide on a large bird, you will be committing yourself to a considerable expenditure of time, of which food preparation is only a relatively small part. Preparing its food each day will become a fairly simple routine, once you get used to it.

The following is intended to give you some idea of what you may experience on a daily basis with a parrot

Left and below: Cockatoos make fine pets, though their talking ability is limited. Shown here is a Lesser Sulphur-crested Cockatoo (left) and a Rose-breasted Cockatoo, or Galah (below). *Opposite:* The Yellow-naped Amazon deserves its reputation for companionability.

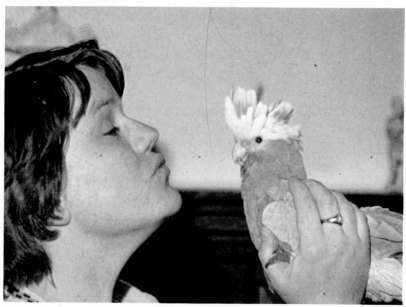

Kelly, the author's harlequin Budgerigar, seems comfortable in the presence of a visiting Senegal Parrot named Alfred.

in your home. Siegfried's daily routine begins at 6:00 AM each morning when our daughter Dawn gives him a fifteen-minute training session before she leaves for school. As is typical of most birds, at this time of day he is the most talkative. His first session with me starts at 8:30 AM, when I attend to his cage. We have some fruit juice and coffee together, and this is blended into a speech-training session. Throughout the day as work permits I spend short periods of time on additional speech training. When left to himself Siegfried may play with his toys, sit and talk to himself, or take little catnaps (excuse the expression). I feed him in the late afternoon, at which time he gets his fresh fruit and vegetables; during the early part of the day he has seed and other dry foods. In the early evening I usually spend a couple of hours playing with him. The evening sessions combine playing, taming, and additional speech training.

Some readers, no doubt, have other pets in the home and quite naturally will be concerned about how a parrot will fit in with the rest of the group. One can always find stories about unusual relationships which develop between very different life forms. My own feeling is that there are always exceptions to expected relationships; in your own home you may succeed in having your dog become pals with a budgie. But you have to decide for yourself if you want to risk one of your pets becoming injured in an accidental confrontation.

In our home we have six cats, a Budgerigar, Siegfried, a turtle, tropical fish, and a parade of "temporary" pets: hamsters, gerbils, etc. When Siegfried arrived on the scene we realized that there was a danger of confrontation with the cats due to his need to be outside of his cage. To reduce the danger of injury to Siegfried and to the cats we have made a point of exposing him and the cats to each other only under carefully controlled conditions. Cats and parrots are very curious about each other, and we realized that the curiosity factor posed the greatest danger. Normally when Siegfried or Kelly (the budgie) are out of their cages, the cats are isolated in other rooms. There are instances when Siegfried and the cats are loose in the same room, but during these times Siegfried is always attended. The idea of letting the cats and Siegfried get used to each other has worked well in that the curiosity has disappeared. Siegfried has made a few unscheduled and unauthorized flights through the house, but the cats have shown no inclination to attack. I would recommend, however, that you keep your pets separated or closely supervised. In our case, I don't believe that the birds and the cats can ever develop a meaningful and lasting relationship, so we keep them apart.

Pet owners in general have a tendency to attribute human qualities to their pets in describing various amus-

Kelly views the drapery rod as her domain and has to be coaxed to come down for lunch.

Opposite:
At the time the author was shopping for a parrot, he found that besides Yellow-napes and Double Yellow-heads, Mealy Amazons (above) and Blue-fronted Amazons (below) were available.

A pen in the author's pocket is too much temptation for Siegfried's mischievous nature. Common items around the home can be selected as toys for parrots. Pens are a good example, but ink tubes and metal pocket clips should be removed first.

ing or interesting events. Parrot owners in particular, and with good reason, are especially enthusiastic in this respect. When the prospective owner reads "intelligent, gregarious, playful, affectionate, excellent mimics, curious," and other such terms, he may be inclined to believe these are exaggerations. If a bird truly possessed all of these qualities, you may feel, that would make it overqualified for most government jobs. Parrots certainly do exhibit enough of these qualities to make them very popular as pets, and they do in all respects become a part of the family.

If you feel inclined toward acquiring a pet parrot and are prepared for some of the time involvement which I have attempted to illustrate, your efforts will be well rewarded. Owning a parrot which is both a good pet and a good talker is a rich experience. At times it will be incredibly amusing, sometimes a bit mule-headed but always challenging and interesting. As I write this section I am listening to one of my favorite operas. Siegfried loves to sing with the soprano; he fluffs out his little facial feathers and sings with great sincerity, several tones off-key.

During the early morning or late afternoon, a normal, healthy bird like Siegfried is particularly active—climbing around its cage, chewing on a toy, or engaging in some other play activity.

Selecting Your Parrot

Making a list of some of your reasons for wanting to own a parrot may help you in your selection. This list can be viewed, then, as a series of expectations. If you have friends who own parrots, by all means consult them and avail yourself of their valuable experience. There are several books available which concentrate on the specific characteristics of the various members of the parrot family. One of these, and in my opinion the most outstanding, is *Parrots and Related Birds* by Bates and Busenbark (T.F.H. Publications). By all means consult your local pet shops, especially those which specialize in birds. Find out who, on the staff, is the bird expert. Tell him (or her) why you are considering a parrot; then listen to his suggestions. After going through this process you will have acquired some good education and will be close to a decision on the species (or subspecies) which interests you most.

Before going shopping for Siegfried I had read about the various kinds of parrots and decided that I wanted an Amazon. The next step was to decide which of the many species of Amazon would most closely enable me to reach my goal of training a bird that would be a good pet and a good talker. This in itself is a tall order because some individual birds may be neither. Some individuals are potentially good pets but not good talkers; others are potentially good talkers but may not become good pets.

Among the Amazons the Yellow-naped, the Mexican Double Yellow-head, the Panama, the Yellow-crowned, and the Tres Marias have excellent reputations for their talking ability. Incidentally, all five mentioned are subspecies of the Yellow-crowned Amazon, *Amazona ochrocephala.* The Blue-fronted *(A. aestiva),* Blue-crowned *(A. farinosa guatemalae),* and Mealy Amazons *(A. f. farinosa)* are also excellent talkers, as are some others. All of these birds are also highly regarded as pets. In fact, the entire genus of Amazon parrots enjoys a reputation for tamability.

The selection of which species to buy is narrowed down for all of us by the availability factor. In my home area I discovered that Yellow-napes, Double Yellow-heads, Blue-fronts, and Mealys were available. To narrow it down still further, only the Double Yellow-heads and the Blue-fronts were available in quantity. Happily, both of these species are included in the five top-rated birds for talking ability. I consider it important that the species you decide upon be available in quantity because

While hand-raising does ensure tameness, it doesn't offer any guarantees about the parrot's other traits.

This seven-week-old Double Yellow-head is the same bird shown opposite with Velma Hart, whose formulas are the basis for current hand-feeding practice.

the toughest part of the decision may be in finding the right individual.

In the course of my shopping I found myself on the premises of a gentleman who is a bird wholesaler. He had about a dozen Double Yellow-heads and maybe six Blue-fronts at the time of my visit. I had already seen a fully mature Double Yellow-head with yellow feathering covering the entire head and neck. The bird had a very impressive and noble appearance, somewhat reminiscent of the Bald Eagle. The memory of seeing that bird caused me to gravitate toward the cages containing the young Double Yellow-heads. These birds were all between six and eight months of age. It is important to you as a trainer to obtain a young bird, preferably less than a year old. One of the advantages of selecting a species which has notable immature plumage characteristics is that the age of the bird can be determined, to within a few months, by immediate observation.

While youth is important, sex is not. It isn't really important which sex your bird is, unless you are a breeder. Most Amazons are not *sexually dimorphic* (there are no outwardly obvious differences between males and females of the same species). In fact, they are so difficult to sex that pet owners often have to arbitrarily decide whether to give them male or female names.

One of the characteristics I have noted about all the Double Yellow-heads I have seen is a boldness when approached by a stranger. Many birds of other species were inclined to retreat to the opposite side of the cage when approached. It's quite understandable, of course, to be a bit wary of a stranger, especially if he is so much bigger than you are. In contrast, the Double Yellow-heads were more inclined to stand their ground and growl. This boldness appealed to me; I felt intuitively that a bird and I were much more likely to get along if we weren't afraid of each other.

As to the selection of Siegfried, that wasn't very difficult at all. All the Double Yellow-heads appeared to be in good health, as I moved from one cage to the next. Siegfried was in the very last cage, and I was immediately taken by a certain look of intelligence as he stared steadily at me and I stared at him. I moved away from the cages and asked the owner which of the Double Yellow-heads he liked best. Without hesitation he pointed to Siegfried. "Why do you think he's the best one?" I asked. "Well, I don't know," he said; "there's just something about him." Well, there it was, hardly a scientific selection. The dealer and myself both made something of an intuitive guess and saw a certain undefinable quality in a bird who was just one of many others.

But there are some very tangible qualities to watch for when you make your selection. Your first consideration should be that the bird is in good health and is eating well. It will save you a lot of time and effort if the dealer has his birds on a well-balanced diet. With the large parrots this must include fresh foods. Look carefully at the plumage; if you see any bare spots, don't buy the bird. Examine the beak to see that it is well formed and that upper and lower mandibles are well fitted. The eyes should be clear and the gaze steady; droopy eyelids or a shifty gaze are not good signs. The nostrils should be fully round and clear. Look at the legs and feet; count the toes. Examine the claws. (I encountered a bird with such a frantic nature that it habitually bit its claws and would literally chew down to the quick, causing bleeding.) The bird should have good body weight, so have the dealer hold the bird while you check this. You should be able to feel that the keel of the sternum (the breastbone) has some meat over it. On either side of the keel the breast should feel good and meaty. You can practice this anatomy lesson by examining the chickens in your local supermarket. You don't want a scrawny parrot.

All reputable dealers will guarantee their birds to be in good health, but if you have doubts about a bird, don't buy it. You might try visiting your prospective pet at the time of day when it is most active, namely, early morning or late afternoon. A healthy, normal bird will be engaged in some activity of play: chewing a stick, climbing around, etc. A listless, moping bird is not a good candidate—but don't judge hastily; it may just be taking an off-schedule nap.

It isn't possible for any of us without medical training to thoroughly judge the health of a bird. As laymen, all we can look for are obvious abnormalities and deformities. It would be a good investment on your part to arrange with the dealer for the bird to have a thorough physical exam by a vet specializing in avian medicine. If the bird is fit, you pay the bill; if he's sick, the dealer pays the bill.

The relationship between a parrot and its owner depends on the individuality of each.

Having discussed the health of the individual, we can now concern ourselves with its individuality. As you'll see later in this volume, the individuality of a bird develops largely as a consequence of its taming, training, and overall relationship with its owner. This isn't to say that the bird has no individuality before it makes friends with a human; it just may not be fully revealed. We are all looking for the marvelously affectionate and talkative pet that we read about, but how can we realistically expect an untamed bird to demonstrate these qualities? A feathered superstar is the result of perhaps years of companionship with a human. Selecting a bird for its potential as an individual is, I'm afraid, as chancy a proposition as selecting your human friends.

There are a few pointers that you might use as a guide; and here again I will focus on Amazons so as not to be too vague.

Whenever approaching a caged bird, do so very slowly and make no rapid hand or head motions.

Good signs: The bird doesn't retreat from you, or retreats slowly. It shows curiosity about you, cocks its head, and gives you an intent one-eyed stare. It greets you with low chirruping sounds or shows interest in your voice. It is eating or playing when you approach, and after examining you it continues the activity. Since it sees a lot of visitors, this means it has a steady nature. You can test the bird as follows: Very slowly bring one of your hands into the bird's view. Move it close to the cage mesh, palm out, fingers extended. Move your hand slowly from one side of the cage to the other, that is across the wall of the cage closest to you. The bird should accept this calmly, but be careful how you do it. You aren't trying to frighten it, which will surely happen if the movement is fast. You just want to see if it has a steady nature.

Bad signs: As you approach, the bird immediately retreats and squawks fearfully. It plasters itself against the far side of the cage. It flutters about the cage in a panicky fashion as if trying to escape your presence. It emits a lot of panicky squawking, objecting to your presence. Don't try the hand test on such birds. If a bird is highly strung, it will be very difficult to tame.

Because of all the factors involved, you can see how selecting a particular bird from a group can be considerably more difficult than deciding which species is right for you. It is hoped that some of the comments and cautions you have read here will assist you.

When you do make your selection, keep in mind that your expectations of the bird must be realistic. One of our local pet stores had a young Double Yellow-head I had become acquainted with during my frequent visits. The owner had tamed the bird, and I heartily concurred with his statement that he was going to be a really nice pet for somebody. Well, sometime after this, the bird was gone, sold to a young couple who wanted a parrot. I remarked that they were very lucky to find such a nice bird, especially since he showed such a friendly disposition. A week later I was surprised to see the Yellow-head back in his old cage. I recognize him by his friendly manner as I approached. "What's Pedro (not the bird's real name) doing back here?" I asked the owner. "The people who bought him said he was too wild for them." I'm sure my astonishment showed, because the owner grinned and said, "Can you believe calling Pedro too wild?"

The message we can take from this incident is that in our relationships with all creatures we must educate ourselves to understand their natures. The young couple truly didn't know what to expect of a pet parrot and didn't recognize Pedro's exceptional nature. I could also add that giving up after only a week tells me those folks weren't much interested in learning.

My own selection of Siegfried as an individual was based on nothing much more tangible than an intuitive guess. You might be as fortunate as the young couple and find a young bird which has already been tamed. However your selection is made, I would recommend, once it has been made, that you give that bird the strength of your conviction that you have found a superstar.

Double Yellow-heads are highly regarded for their talking abilities, but I find not much written on their character. From direct contact with owners and dealers the consensus is that Double Yellow-heads "typically" are very active and playful, somewhat aggressive, not likely to be timid, easily tamed, more inclined to bite than some species, and enjoy human company. If this description is reasonably accurate for the species, then Siegfried is most certainly a typical specimen. I have heard of and observed some Double Yellow-heads which are gentle and affectionate pets. Yet individuals of any species may develop nontypical characteristics, and in its many moods any bird may display behavior not typical of its usual self. Siegfried has all of the traits listed above, including being affectionate, but I would hesitate to describe his boisterous play as gentle. He is usually gentle when he's not in a playful mood.

Parrots have very strong personalities as a general rule, as distinct from one bird to the next as from one human to another. This is the factor which makes parrots so unpredictable in taming and training situations. Siegfried is very much inclined toward speech and other fun sounds but is not at all inclined toward physical tricks. I have been trying to get him to learn a particular simple little trick for about four or five months without success. I use these points to illustrate that your parrot won't necessarily learn speech or tricks merely because the *trainer* thinks it's a good idea. *The parrot* also has to think it's a good idea—and because parrots are pretty smart, they learn very quickly to put their good ideas into practice.

The reader will, I hope, grasp that attempting to describe the various attributes of such intelligent birds as the members of the parrot family and to place these characteristics into neat niches for future reference is as risky as trying to describe the typical human from South Dakota. Each bird is an individual, with all that the term *individuality* conveys.

A transport cage can be very useful for putting your parrot outside for some fresh air, taking him to the vet or taking him away with you on vacation.

Housing and Equipment

The first consideration, after you have decided on what kind of parrot you want, is a suitable cage. I don't personally like the word *cage* because it conveys imprisonment, but I'm afraid we're stuck with it.

There is a wide selection of cages available at your local pet store, and they are all designed to provide comfortable homes. Obviously they come in all shapes and sizes, so it's just a matter of selecting the correct size for your bird. Siegfried's cage is a somewhat ornamental affair which was made in Mexico. The larger Amazons need lots of room, so a good-sized cage should be about twenty-four inches square on the bottom and about thirty-six inches high. Parrots enjoy climbing up and down more than travelling horizontally, so a tall cage is preferable.

I prefer natural tree branches for perches over the standard dowels. Branches give a bird an irregularity of shape which is good for its feet. If you choose to replace the perches already there with natural branches, make them about one and one-half inches in diameter. Leave the bark on the branch so the bird can chew it off himself. Birds as a general rule like to roost in the highest places of their environment. This is certainly true of parrots. You don't want to clutter up its air space in the cage, but I would recommend a sleeping perch. It needs to be no longer than about six inches, and one and one-half inches in diameter—a small piece of tree branch will be perfect. Find a way to mount this to one wall of the cage, as high as possible, leaving just

Siegfried's cage is well suited for an Amazon parrot, especially if the bird is allowed to spend part of the day out of its cage.

The stub perch is Siegfried's favorite place. Family members refer to this as "Siegfried's office." All the most delicious treats are taken up to his office to be eaten with great care, for maximum enjoyment.

enough headroom for the bird in its sleeping posture. Siegfried and I gradually developed this idea of the "stub perch" by trying various plans for the decor of his home.

What I will call the "main perch" is located near the floor of the cage. It is high enough for Siegfried's tail to have a couple of inches of clearance from the floor. The main perch runs the full width of the cage and food dishes are placed at each end, mounted on the cage mesh. This arrangement provides a larger airy space in the middle for the bird to fully extend his wings.

When you buy your cage, it will probably be equipped with food dishes. You may need to add to these so that you have a water dish, a seed dish, a fresh-food dish, and a small dish for health grit. The cage should also contain a large mineral block, which can be mounted on the mesh. All dishes should be securely mounted so that the bird can't upset them.

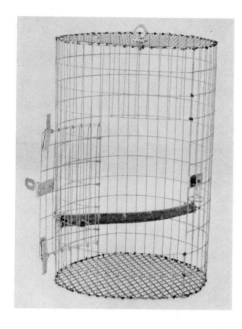

The eye bolt on the transport cage is useful for hanging, and the hinged clasp allows you to secure the door. A cage such as this is simple and efficient for the purpose.

An Amazon should be allowed to spend some time outside of its cage. Many owners like to just open the cage and let the bird climb up on top. As an alternative you can obtain a floor stand, or make one yourself. The stand shown in the photo is homemade. Notice that the perch arrangement is made from tree branches.

If you feel the need for a small holding cage for your bird, such as for transporting it, you can make one quite inexpensively. At your local feed or hardware store buy some 1 x 2-inch welded wire mesh. With this material you can make a small cage as shown in the photo. One more item you can make yourself (or buy) is a small tabletop stand. This can be useful in speech-training sessions. I would suggest making the perch high enough so that your bird cannot easily climb down.

All the cages you will see offered for sale feature a pull-out tray at the bottom, for cleaning. Often, above the tray, there is a floor of mesh that the bird walks on. With this type of design, droppings fall through the

Play stands for parrots typically have a surface below the perch to catch food and droppings. Some have food cups as well, so the bird may be kept on the stand for longer periods. As chewing is likely, wooden parts should be replaceable. Note here that the uppermost perch is purposely very short to allow for wing-flapping exercises.

mesh so that they will be out of the way of the bird. The only problem I see with this is that everything else falls through too: his small toys, the kernel from a peanut he was carefully shelling, and many other choice bits of his lunch.

The nicest display of parrots offered for sale I've seen is in one of our local pet stores in Albuquerque. It consists of several large glass-fronted showcases, in which small trees "grow" up from the floor. They are well lighted, and the floors are covered to a depth of two to three inches with wood shavings. I was especially impressed by this display because at the time of my visit one of the many showcases contained two young Mexican Double Yellow-heads. They were frolicking about on the floor like a couple of puppies. One of them occasionally rolled over on its back and played with a stick with both feet and beak. The showcases were meticulously clean, and the birds quite obviously were healthy and happy.

It is while he is in his office (on the stub perch) that Siegfried does his speech homework—practicing phrases by himself and sometimes shuffling words to make new phrases.

The best place in your home to keep your parrot is the room in which your family spends the most time together. It will see itself as part of the family; and when it learns to talk, it will join in the conversation. The African Grey shown here is obviously "lord of the manor"—he owns two very nice humans named Max and Gloria Mills.

I immediately bought a large bag of wood shavings from the proprietor and converted Siegfried's cage. If you want to consider this method you will need some cardboard to cover your present floor mesh, or perhaps you can remove it. You will also need some stout clear plastic or some other material to cover the bottom four or five inches of wall mesh; this will prevent the shavings from falling out. Cleaning the cage can be accomplished by using a tissue to remove any droppings that you see during your visits.

Siegfried has become well adjusted to the arrangement and can retrieve the food which he frequently drops. He especially seems to enjoy foraging in the shavings in the early morning to find the peanuts from the previous day. I feel confident about recommending this set-up because it brings a bit more natural environment to your parrot.

Siegfried's well-balanced diet helps keep him a well-balanced parrot.

Daily Care

Cleaning

Your first responsibility to your pet is to keep it healthy and happy, and it will be neither unless you take care of this chore every day. I would suggest that your first job each morning should be to remove the overnight droppings and stale food remnants from the bottom of the cage. Your parrot is a clean bird, but it needs your help to stay clean. If it has to walk about in its own soil, you aren't going to want it to sit on your shoulder. If it smells, you won't want to play with it, and it will develop into a sad little bird with no friends.

Please keep its cage spotlessly clean at all times. Any time you see droppings in its food or water, please clean the dishes thoroughly and replace the contents. When your bird becomes accustomed to its new home, it will develop some habits of movement around its cage. It will eventually put most droppings in a certain area of the cage. When you see the habit develop, adjust the locations of food dishes and lower perches to avoid unnecessary fouling.

Periodically take your friend out of its cage and scrub it from top to bottom—the cage, that is; we'll talk about scrubbing your friend later. Clean or scrape any mess off the perches and remove any dried food remnants from the cage mesh. Follow the advice of your bird dealer regarding the use of any disinfectants and parasite treatments.

As you clean the cage each morning, give your attention to the condition of the droppings. A healthy bird will produce fecal matter which is dark green in color and of solid consistency. There will also be the white urine of pasty consistency and clear fluid. The amount of fluid will depend on the bird's diet. If it has been eating only dry foods then there will be less fluid than if it is eating a fair amount of fresh food. I call your attention to this, because any significant change from the healthy droppings described could mean a health problem. If at any time you do observe a change, call your vet.

Feeding

It is commonly known that birds have a high metabolism rate. They consume a considerable quantity of food each day to maintain a high body temperature, not to mention such other high-energy uses as flying. The larger parrots are notable in their needs for considerable food bulk and variety in order to maintain good health. When you buy your parrot you should inquire about what it is accustomed to eating, then purchase a supply of that particular mix. In addition to this, determine from the many reference books available the correct diet for that species. If you decide on a large parrot such as an Amazon it is quite possible that the dealer has been feeding only a dry-food mix. When you get this bird home, in addition to taming it you will have to introduce it to fresh foods. I cannot overemphasize the absolute necessity for good nutrition in your new pet. As has often been found to be the case in human beings, many health and behavioral problems in parrots can be traced to poor nutrition.

Give the bird a few days to settle in before making drastic changes in its diet. The move to a new home is obviously somewhat upsetting, and your major consideration about food should be that it continues to eat well. Once you're sure it hasn't lost his appetite, in-

An Amazon's dry-food needs can be filled by using one of the many commercially prepared seed mixes available at your local pet shop.

troduce the new foods. With Amazons the easiest fresh food to start on is chunks of apple. (Remove the pits from all fruits that you serve because many, especially apple pits, contain toxic cyanides.) The bird will most likely need some time to adjust to the new foods. If it doesn't take to them immediately, don't give up, for it must not be allowed to reject this essential part of its diet. Siegfried accepted some items—such as apples, pears, grapes, and cucumber—after just a few days. Other items—carrots, oranges, and cabbage—took weeks. The process of educating your bird to the new foods will vary, of course, depending on the bird. I found that with some foods I could just place them in the fresh-food dish every day. Eventually the bird would begin accepting them. In other instances, with a stubborn bird, for example, persistent offering by hand may be necessary. Keep in mind that for Amazons a major part of their natural diet is fresh greens and fruits, so don't let your bird convince you otherwise. Humans are responsible for its present incorrect diet; it's up to us now to correct the mistake.

When I first bought Siegfried he was approximately seven months old, which in parrot terms is infancy. He had apparently been living on an exclusively seed diet for some time because he seemed unfamiliar with and disinterested in fresh foods. In the course of correcting this I found it necessary to use a variety of tricks and subterfuges to help him acquire a taste for certain foods. To illustrate:

Cheese is a good source of fats, calcium, and protein, but for two or three weeks Siegfried ignored his daily ration. I switched the type of cheese to an orange-colored Cheddar (orange, red, and bright yellows are parrots' favorite colors) and he immediately began eating it. Now he will eat cheese of any color.

Bananas are also very good for Amazons, but as it

A vitamin supplement is necessary to help maintain a parrot's good health. Many such supplements can simply be dissolved in your pet's drinking water.

A mineral block is a source of trace elements, and it can also help keep your parrot's beak in good condition.

turned out Siegfried wouldn't pick up anything in his foot if it was wet or sticky to the touch. I solved this by serving his banana with the skin still on. He gets a piece cut off the end of the fruit and will happily hold it and eat the insides out of the little cuplike shape.

I find that once a bird acquires the taste for the food, I can revert to a more ordinary way of feeding. Be watchful of what your bird is leaving in its dish and attempt to discover why it won't eat certain items. If you can't persuade it to eat certain foods, don't be afraid to switch to something else that will provide the equivalent nutrition. The main consideration with your bird is that it have the normal, healthy appetite which is necessary to support its high metabolism.

Recommended Diet for Amazons. In captivity Amazon parrots, from analysis and the experience of many aviculturists, should be fed a daily diet as follows. *Dry food:* Budgerigar seed mix, safflower and

Like a scene from *Oliver Twist*, Siegfried seems to be asking for his food dish to be refilled. The small dish seen in the background holds health grit which contains crushed oyster shells and other minerals.

sunflower seeds, wheat germ, brewer's yeast, dry dog food, raw peanuts (unsalted), walnuts and other nuts. In daily practice you can feed a "parrot mix" obtainable from your pet store to accommodate his dry-food needs. *Fresh food:* apples, pears, oranges, grapes, bananas, etc.; carrots, celery, cabbage, corn, cucumber, etc. In his fresh-food dish, feed him two kinds of fresh fruit and one yellow and one green vegetable each day. Lastly, use a water-soluble vitamin supplement.

Siegfried's Daily Diet. This is *based* on the experts' recommendations. Like so many parrots Siegfried has his own likes and dislikes. We have managed to persuade him to eat certain foods (fresh fruits) which he wouldn't touch as a baby. There are some other foods (small seeds) which he steadfastly refuses to have anything to do with. At present his daily diet is as follows. *Dry food:* About two tablespoons of sunflower seed, 6–8 raw peanut kernels, two or three pieces of dry

Siegfried is fed once a day, and his food remains in the cage until it is replaced the following day. There is no set pattern to his eating habits, except that he is likely to eat at any time during his waking hours. At any given time, usually only small amounts of food are taken, but there are occasions when he has worked up an appetite and eats heartily when fresh food is served.

cat food, and one monkey-chow cookie. Siegfried is more likely to eat the monkey chow if it has been soaked in water for a few seconds. Lastly, some lay pellets (dried vegetables) are added. *Fresh food* (I will use the term *cube*—roughly sugar-cube size or one cubic centimeter—to give an idea of daily quantities): 3 cubes cheese, 4 cubes orange (1 slice), 8 cubes apple, 4 cubes pear, 4 cubes banana, 2 grapes, 2 cubes celery, 2 cubes carrot, 1 cube turnip, 2 cubes cabbage—all sprinkled with one-half teaspoon brewer's yeast; walnuts and Brazil nuts as treats. Finally, vitamins in his drinking water.

Many reference books indicate that a parrot's daily diet should include some form of grit (gravel) to aid the digestive process. This is based on the presumption that since birds have no teeth they therefore cannot chew their food. Chickens and some other seedeaters do swallow their food, husk and all. These birds ingest small particles of grit which helps to grind the food for full digestion.

My study of Siegfried has shown that at least one parrot "chews" his food very thoroughly. Each bite of food is held by the tongue against the ridged inside surface of the upper mandible while the cutting edge of the lower mandible shaves it into a fine mush. Siegfried has a small dish of health grit in his cage and a large mineral block mounted high on the cage mesh. Although these have always been available to him, at no time have I ever seen him use them.

Dr. Timothy L. Fitzpatrick, who specializes in avian medicine, informed me that in his opinion the use of grit for parrots is "overdone." He feels that grit should be offered only about once a week. He added that some of his feathered patients, when overly excited, have eaten too much grit and developed problems as a consequence.

Plumage

Most people during some period in their lives have developed a familiarity with such typical household pets as cats and dogs. This leads us quite naturally to other fur- or hair-covered mammals in our choice of pets. We remind ourselves that we humans too are hair-covered mammals.

If the reader has recently acquired a parrot or is considering the purchase—and especially if this is your first experience with birds—it is very appropriate that you learn something about their feathers.

The word *plumage* is used to encompass the various types of feathers, which serve many functions. To minimize confusion we will focus on the Amazon parrots for a detailed description. The feathers we see when a bird is in flight or perched vary in size, from a fraction of an inch for the smallest facial and shoulder feathers up to several inches for the primary wing feathers. For ease of understanding I'll subdivide these feathers further and describe their functions.

Body feathers: These cover the face, head, neck, torso, and legs. These are softly structured feathers that overlap to such an extent that only a small percentage of the overall length is actually visible. Body feathers vary in size and shape depending on where they are located. They provide warmth and protect the delicate skin from the elements and physical injury. Another very important function they provide is the aerodynamic smoothness of contour for flight.

Wing feathers: The largest feathers of the Amazon parrot are the *primaries* of the wing. The skeletal structure of the wing is generally comparable to the human arm. What is commonly called the "bend of the wing" or "shoulder" of a bird corresponds to the human wrist. The primary flight feathers grow from the bird's "hand." There are ten primaries on each wing, and they

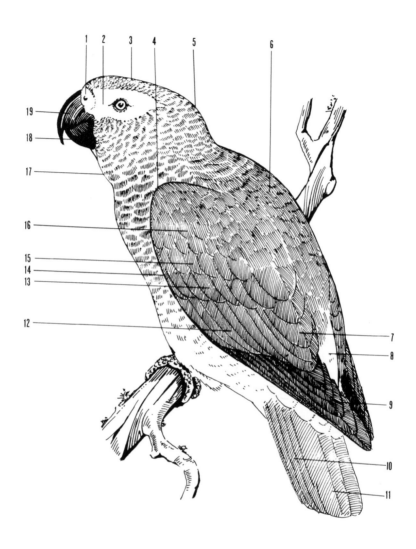

Topography of a parrot:
1, cere; *2*, lores; *3*, crown; *4*, bend of wing; *5*, nape; *6*, mantle; *7*, tertials; *8*, rump; *9*, primaries; *10*, Lateral tail feathers; *11*, central tail feathers; *12*, secondaries; *13*, greater wing coverts; *14*, carpal edge of the wing; *15*, median wing coverts; *16*, lesser wing coverts; *17*, throat; *18*, lower mandible; *19*, upper mandible.

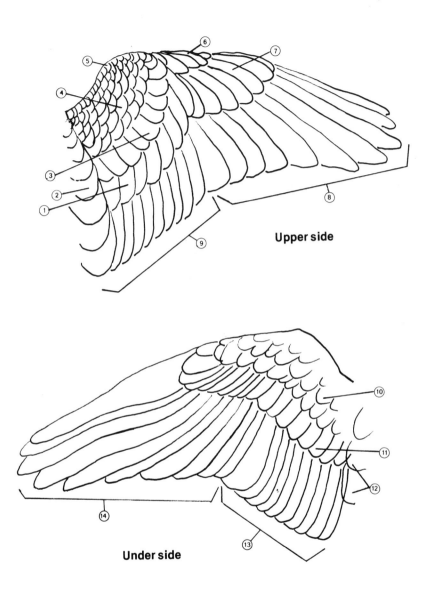

Upper side

Under side

Parts of a parrot's wing:
1, secondary coverts; *2*, tertials; *3*, median wing coverts; *4*, lesser wing coverts; *5*, bend of wing; *6*, carpal edge; *7*, primary coverts; *8*, primaries; *9*, secondaries; *10*, lesser under wing coverts; *11*, greater under wing coverts; *12*, axillaries; *13*, secondaries; *14*, primaries.

are characteristically long and slim, quite stiff and slightly curved. The *secondaries* grow from the bird's "forearm." They are noticeably shorter and broader than the primaries and less stiff; they are also curved. Parrots have ten secondaries to each wing. *Tertial* feathers are arranged perpendicularly to the length of the wing—in other words, parallel to the bird's body length. They don't have the stiffness to qualify as flight feathers but do serve to stiffen the wing at the base by overlapping each other. *Primary and secondary coverts* have the characteristic stiff structure of functional flight feathers. They grow from the "hand" and "forearm" and extend over the primary and secondary flight feathers. These coverts serve to control the flexing of the longer feathers. There are several other groups of wing coverts which overlap each other on the top and underside of the wing. These many rows of feathers not only give strength and stiffness to the wing but also provide aerodynamic camber.

Tail feathers: Amazon parrots all have rather short tails composed of twelve feathers. Two of these are *central* tail feathers that can be easily identified when they molt because of their straightness. The other ten are *laterals,* and these feathers, five on each side of the central pair, curve inward slightly, giving the tail a tapered shape. Tail feathers are stiff and serve to stabilize the body attitude in flight. They also aid in maneuvering through turns, add lift during takeoffs, and aid deceleration for landing. In flight and sometimes while playing in its cage the Amazon spreads the tail feathers in a colorful fanlike array. During his last molt Siegfried very generously contributed a complete set of the major wing and tail feathers to our research.

Down feathers: They are hidden from view beneath the body feathers; they cover much of the body and provide insulation against the cold and vary in density depending on whether the bird is kept indoors or in an outside aviary. They will also vary for an aviary bird at various times of the year. Your bird will adjust the density of its down feathers by molting out or growing new feathers to meet its needs. When you find a down feather in your bird's cage, it will appear at first glance to be a nondescript little ball of fluff. If you examine it under a magnifier, however, you will see a remarkable sight. The ball of fluff is transformed into an intricate little shrub. The quill is short and squat; emanating from it in all directions are several fernlike fronds. Each of the delicate fronds has a long central stem from which grow tiny hairs in great profusion. The hairs are long at the base of the stem, gradually becoming shorter in length as the frond tapers to a point. *Powder-down* feathers are in a continual process of growth, as their delicate fronds continually disintegrate into a fine powder. While the bird is preening, the beak receives some of the powder, which is transferred to other feathers and serves to clean and groom them.

Feather Growth

When feathers begin to grow, they exit, encased in a soft sheath, from a follicle in the bird's skin. In the case of some smaller feathers the sheath actually bends the new feather into a curl. As growth continues, the stiff sheath pushes the feather up through the other plumage. During the course of preening, the parrot finds the new feathers and nibbles away at the sheath, allowing the feather to "bloom." The removal of the sheath is not necessarily accomplished in one operation but continues bit by bit until the feather is fully grown. When your bird is tame enough to allow it, probe gently among its feathers until you find a new one. You will notice it easily enough by the stiffness of the sheath. Sometimes a

A table stand with a sufficiently large base to prevent upsetting (nine by fifteen inches works fine) can be useful during taming, training, and spray bathing. The perch on this stand is the scrap end of a drapery rod, and the other parts are just scrap lumber.

Opposite:
Above: A stout, full-length lower perch provides a comfortable, natural footing for the bird and allows convenient access to food and water. The thick bed of shavings adds to the parrot's play area, provides a soft cushion if he takes a fall, and improves cage cleanliness. *Below:* The spring retainer keeps the food dish in place; the hooks are made from stout wire. For some birds this precaution is not necessary. Siegfried, however, will move, remove, or upset anything that isn't secure. He was able to unhook the spring until I eventually learned to stretch it diagonally instead of vertically.

Mutual preening is a common courtship activity among parrots—these are Cockatiels.

neck feather, for example, will be in bloom at the outer end while as much as three quarters of an inch of the remainder is still sheathed. All growing feathers are referred to as "blood feathers." This is because the feather is fed by blood located in the quill. When growth is complete, the blood supply atrophies (and the feather can be safely clipped, if needed, without bleeding).

It is generally assumed that when a young bird grows its first feathers it has a full complement, just like an adult. This would have to be true for the flight feathers, but it isn't necessarily true for the body feathers. When Siegfried was approximately eight months old and seemingly in full feather, he suddenly sprouted a new crop on his lower and midneck region. Another observation which I will describe supports my suggestion that on immature birds the attainment of full feathering is a gradual process.

The immature Mexican Double Yellow-head has yellow feathers only on the forehead and maybe extending slightly onto the crown. During a three-to-five year period the yellow increases until it covers the entire head and neck. Molting and refeathering, with yellow feathers replacing green, is apparently credited for the process. I have studied this change carefully in Siegfried's case, taking photographs of his head each month and making notes on the gradual increase of yellow head feathers. In no instance has he lost a green feather, yet many new yellow feathers have appeared. Some new feathers on the head are bicolored, yellow and green. I believe further study of young birds should be undertaken before firm conclusions can be drawn. Perhaps the observations recorded here will prompt bird owners to contribute their own observations.

Preening

This is the process by which your parrot takes care of its plumage. In the process it transfers powder from some down feathers to clean other feathers. It takes oil from a gland on its rump near the base of its tail and uses this to dress the major feathers of wings and tail. You may have noticed a slight waxiness or oiliness as you touch its back. While it is preening, it will sometimes come away with a feather in its beak. Don't be alarmed at this; it doesn't mean your bird is plucking itself—down feathers particularly are often removed in this manner. If your bird comes out from under its wing with a large flight feather I would suggest taking the feather out of the cage. Your bird will probably just drop the feather to the floor of the cage anyway, but if it is having a slow day, it may decide to play with the feather for a while,and that could become a bad habit. Preening is done with the beak, which can reach all parts of the body except the head (the claws are used to

Siegfried is preening his flight feathers. Some parrots, both in captivity and in the wild, carry this behavior to an extreme.

Opposite:
This Scarlet Macaw has
plucked its breast bare.

scratch the head and facial feathers). Your bird may seem to spend a lot of its time preening, but again there is usually no need for concern. Parrots are endowed by nature with the most beautiful plumage of all birds, and it takes a lot of their time to keep it looking nice. When I am asked by friends of the family or visitors if parrots are messy pets, I use preening as an example of their desire for cleanliness.

Feather Plucking

If you have bought a healthy bird without any bare spots in its plumage and it is eating properly, there is little likelihood that you will experience this problem. My study of various references and conversations with bird dealers indicates that tension, boredom, poor diet, or parasites are the principal causes. As previously mentioned, there is not usually any need for concern if your bird seems to be preoccupied with its plumage. Many new pet owners unaccustomed to the amount of time the bird spends on this chore tend to become alarmed prematurely. It is wise of course and quite natural that you will be interested in the welfare of your pet. If you are really worried, call your bird dealer and discuss the problem.

Broken Feathers

The normal, healthy parrot is an active bird. When not eating, preening, or sleeping it will be engaged in play. Parrots love to perform acrobatics and climb around the cage to show off. Once in a while Siegfried gets a little bit carried away and while hanging up-sidedown will let go first with one foot, then the other. Needless to say, this can be a bit rough on his plumage. Tail feathers are especially prone to damage because even in a good-sized cage they are in frequent contact with the wire mesh. If a tail feather gets poked through the mesh, it may get broken as the parrot places strain upon it. If the feather is fully grown (not a blood feather), then there is little cause for concern. You can try straightening it out, if the shaft hasn't actually cracked, and this may be all that is necessary. If, however, it wants to stay stuck out at an odd angle, then it is best to just clip it off. Experienced bird owners and professionals prefer to extract the broken feather—the operative word here is *experienced*. If you and your bird are new to each other, cutting the feather will be less traumatic for you both. The stub will eventually be molted and replaced. If the broken feather is still growing, then there is a possibility of bleeding. I say *possibility* because unless the quill actually ruptures, even a blood feather won't bleed. In this instance it is best to have the feather extracted by an experienced bird dealer. A bent-out, broken feather will be especially susceptible to further damage, so by all means attend to it. The most common and almost inevitable form of feather damage you will see is called "cage whipping." This is nothing more than the shredding of the ends of the feathers—usually the tail feathers—by frequent dragging across the mesh of the cage. I find that bathing temporarily restores the appearance of these feathers. They usually have lost some of the fine "hairs" (barbs) which make up the web of the feathers. Most of the disheveled tattered look is the result of web separation. When your bird takes a bath, be sure it gets its tail good and wet. When you spot this condition on your bird, it doesn't necessarily mean the cage is too small. It is, however, part of keeping a bird in a cage. Some individual Amazons are very particular about their tails, and with these birds the tail feathers always look immaculate. Young birds, like young children, are more interested in rough-and-tumble fun.

The first step in the bathing procedure is to assemble bird and materials in an area with all unnecessary items cleared away. Here Siegfried reaches for the spray bottle, maybe to give it one good bite before it is used on him.

Opposite:
Above: Siegfried is so accustomed to his baths that he now opens his wings as soon as he begins to feel the spray. *Below:* A bird must be thoroughly tamed and have considerable confidence in its owner before it can be expected to perform antics like this. Siegfried wants to be sure that we wash behind his ears.

Molting

In his book *Parrots of the World* (T.F.H. Publications), Joseph M. Forshaw shows that considerable study has been done on the subject. My main objective here is simply to note that molting (the shedding and replacement of feathers) will occur about once a year and to explain the process in general terms. If you've just bought your little friend and then get up one morning to find a lot of feathers on the floor of its cage, you might tend to think that your parrot is becoming unraveled. Before coming across Mr. Forshaw's book I had been already studying the process and was interested and relieved to find my observations confirmed as typical. Siegfried started to molt in the month of November, at the age of approximately eight months. A few body feathers were molted first, followed by the loss of a primary. It was quite interesting to note that the primaries are molted symmetrically: one from the right wing, then one from the left. This particular observation was made easy for me by the fact that at the time all his primaries on one wing were clipped. I was finding one stub, then one full feather, etc. The process is very slow, so a complete molt lasts for several months. It typically starts with the loss of a primary; then, I noticed, another primary is lost after two or three days. After a couple of weeks, another primary; then, two or three days after that, the primary from the other wing drops. All during the molting period the bird's ability to fly is undiminished. Siegfried's tail feathers all molted within about six weeks, but at no time did he appear tailless. These feathers apparently molt during a shorter period than do wing feathers. Molting does not necessarily entail the loss of every single feather on your bird. The molt of body feathers, wing coverts, and tail coverts seems to vary in extent.

Siegfried has not exhibited any especially unusual

behavior during his molt, and I suspect that this is typical of a well-nourished, healthy pet. I won't dwell on any special care that you should bestow on your pet during molting because I don't believe it necessary. You are feeding him a well-balanced diet, he is secure and well cared for, and that's all he needs.

Bathing

Whenever I see little finches and sparrows out on the lawn bathing in the sprinklers and chattering away, I wonder why Siegfried doesn't like the idea of taking a bath. Your parrot should bathe regularly and probably will have to be taught how. You can take a shallow dish, place some wet greens in it, add a little water, and—presto!—your bird will take bath.

The first time I tried this I took the precaution of placing the shallow dish in the bathtub. It was wintertime so we couldn't go outside. Siegfried eyed all the paraphenalia with suspicion, walked up on to my shoulder, and refused to come down. I leaned over the tub and sloshed my hands about in the greens so he could see how much fun I was having. Other than to lean forward and give the single-eyed scrutiny of great curiosity, he remained unmoved and immovable. On another occasion I placed the pan in the bathtub first, pried the reluctant bird off my arm, and perched him on the edge. He remained calm as I added some water but revolted violently when I tried to mix parrot and water together. For a time it looked like Siegfried was going to be a permanent member of the ranks of the unwashed. He seemed to take the view that ducks and geese are waterfowl, but parrots are arboreal, frolicking finches notwithstanding.

One day in the pet store I discussed the problem with the proprietor. He also had a pet parrot with the same

Siegfried turns and extends his wing broadside for spraying. He is completely relaxed and obviously having a good time.

Opposite:
Above: When he was younger, Siegfried wouldn't even consider turning his back to the spray bottle; now he seems interested in every feather getting its share of the spray. *Below:* Spray bathing will reward you with many colorful and playful displays.

If provided with a shallow dish with a small bit of water in it, some parrots will bathe by themselves, as this lovebird is doing.

aversion to bathing. He showed me a product called Feather Glo which can be used to give the bird a spray bath. The spray claims to be good for the feathers, and the proprietor said his bird "doesn't mind" being sprayed. Well, this sounded encouraging so I dashed home, grabbed Siegfried, and took him into the bathroom. I set him on the table stand, which is usually used for speech training, and began to spray him with the Feather Glo. He was not enthusiastic, and I got nipped a couple of times when I got too close. Eventually his protests died down, and he began to open up so I could spray his underwings. I used the spray against the direction of feather growth in order to get down all the way to the skin. While I sprayed, he began beating his wings slowly and turning about. I won't go so far as to say that Siegfried now looks forward to his baths. He tolerates them with good grace and will actually talk to me while I spray him. After the first bath I put him back in his cage still very wet, which is a bad idea. Your pet is more likely to catch a cold, and even in a sizable cage he may not have as much room as he would like to flap himself dry. Since the first shower I have used a hair dryer, the pistol-shaped type, to blow him dry. With a hot-air setting and the dryer far enough away so that he doesn't feel an uncomfortable amount of heat, he is completely dry in just a few minutes.

Bathing is an important part of your bird's care. Its plumage will have an added brilliance which is not seen among nonbathers. Try the standard procedure for bathing first, but whatever it takes, convince your bird that in polite society even arboreals are expected to bathe.

Claw Clipping

Occasionally, as you feel your parrot's claws getting too sharp, you will need to clip them. If you haven't done it before, you may prefer to take your bird to the pet store. Claw clipping really isn't a difficult job, provided your bird is fairly tame. I find I can do the job without assistance in just a few minutes. I perch Siegfried on the small table stand and give him a treat to nibble on. While he holds the treat in one foot, I work on the other one. I gently pull one claw slightly away from the perch and, holding it very firmly against his pull, I clip just a small amount off the very tip with ordinary nail clippers. Using this method you have to keep track of which claws you have clipped and which leg you are working on. Your bird may turn around several times and put the treat in the other foot, but if you work very carefully he won't even know what you've done. If you hear an angry squawk, it will mean you clipped too

Now thoroughly soaked, Siegfried alternates between letting the warm air from the dryer blow through his plumage and shaking himself vigorously to throw out the moisture.

Opposite:
Above: The soft body feathers and down take longer to dry because of their absorbency. The dryer does a good job of restoring lost body heat while drying the torso. *Below:* When Siegfried is thoroughly dry, the full color of his plumage will return, and his body feathers will be soft and silky.

Clipping Siegfried's claws causes no discomfort and usually attracts only casual curiosity.

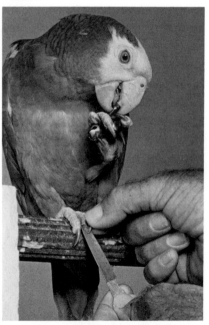

It is advisable to file the claws after clipping to round off the sharp edges which may otherwise result in scratches on the pet owner.

Styptic powder contracts the tissues or blood vessels so that bleeding is quickly stopped.

much. You may see bleeding—have some Quik-Stop (powdered styptic) handy and press it into the end of the claw. When you finish clipping, use a nail file to smooth the rough ends.

Wing Clipping

If you intend to keep your pet in a nonflying condition its wings will need to be clipped at least once a year. The clipped feather stubs drop out when the bird molts, and the new feathers when fully grown restore the bird's ability to fly.

There are two basic styles of wing clipping, and each experienced bird handler has his own preference. The most common style entails clipping all primary and secondary flight feathers down to the coverts of one wing. The less common entails clipping only the primaries of both wings. With both styles sometimes the outermost two primaries are left unclipped for the sake of the bird's appearance.

His after-bath preening completed, Siegfried turns his attention elsewhere.

Opposite:
By spending time with your bird each day, its tameness will develop, and it will feel quite secure and comfortable perched on your wrist. Wing clipping will be unnecessary.

Your parrot can be entertained in hundreds of ways. Rope climbing provides lots of fun and good exercise.

Needless to say, clipping the wing feathers is a job for the expert. I would suggest that you let a professional at your pet store or your vet do it the first time. After that, if you think you and another family member are competent enough to do it without hurting yourselves or the bird, then perhaps you can attempt it.

Toys

Parrots have a high level of intelligence and are physically active during a large portion of the day. They like to be well provided with swings, bells, ropes, and other toys to keep them busy. Because there are hundreds of odds and ends around the house that will do just fine, toys don't have to be an expense item. One thing I would suggest you buy at the pet store, though, is a stout little bell on a chain. Check that the clapper is securely mounted. An empty thread spool and the plastic barrel of a pen (with insert and any small hard-

The piece of rope here facilitates in-cage acrobatics.

A parrot's inborn agility makes it a natural tightrope walker. If you want your bird to make its own way from cage to play stand, try connecting them with a length of rope.

Opposite:
Extending a wing for a prolonged stretch
is a common parrot exercise.

ware removed) can serve as toys, as can short sticks from tree pruning, scrap lumber blocks, etc. Be sure that you give your parrot nothing that is painted or coated with toxic materials. Parrots know the difference between eating and chewing, so don't be concerned about it swallowing wood splinters, etc. These odds and ends may not last too long because the bird will chew on them until they are reduced to fragments. But this occupation is very beneficial to a healthy bird, so before you leave the house each morning check to see that your pet has some toys.

In using a claw for holding food or other objects, parrots are predominantly "left-handed." In the case of Amazon parrots, the incidence of left-handedness is approximately 70%. When engaged in a lengthy chewing project, such as reducing a thread spool to fragments, Siegfried will change "hands" occasionally to rest the supporting leg.

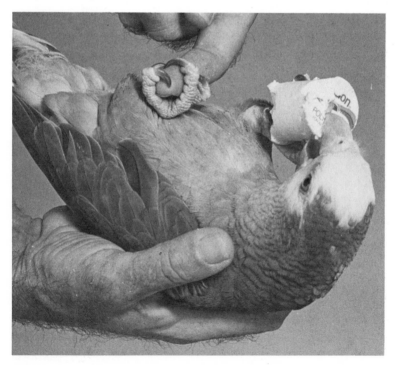

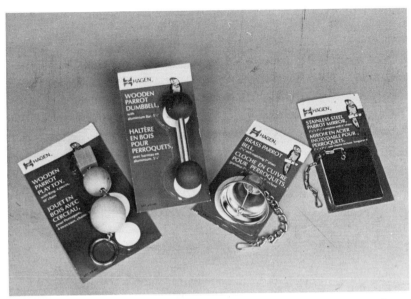

At your local pet shop, there are a variety of toys made especially for the larger parrots.

Play Sessions

I am referring now to play sessions between you and the bird. It is of paramount importance to a good relationship that you take your bird out of its cage and play with it every day. The nature of the Amazon makes it a marvelous pet, but it is demanding of your time and attention. If it doesn't get the attention it needs, it may develop the bad habit of screaming for it. It may also develop meanness and forbid anybody to touch it. In this important respect owning an Amazon is unlike owning many other types of pets. It has to be your "hobby," and I would say conservatively that it needs one to two hours of your time, training and playing with it, each day. If this amount of time isn't available in your life, then owning an Amazon is probably not a good idea.

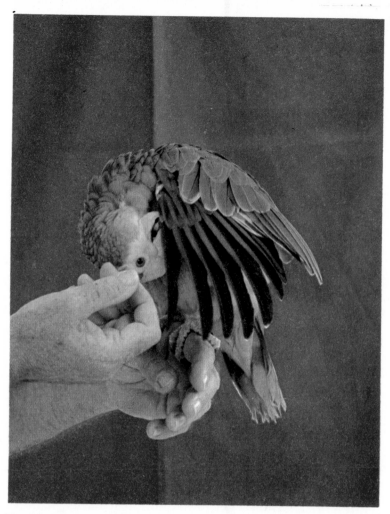

Siegfried shows confidence in his trainer by preening while perched on his trainer's hand.

Opposite:
A bundle of primaries; a bundle of secondaries, showing the red speculum; a greenish blue primary covert; a yellow head feather; a tiny red covert from the bend of the wing; a large greenish body feather.

If you and your feathered pet are to have a companionable relationship, you must take the time to tame it.

Taming

It never ceases to surprise me when I hear of a situation where a person buys a parrot with the object of taming it and teaching it to talk and then gives up almost before he gets started. The pet owner may experience a couple of hard bites, so he decides to quit handling the bird. The owner may have read that some birds don't like to be handled and misapplies this to his own situation so the bird does not become tame. Interestingly, I have encountered situations where an untamed bird is treated to a surprisingly consistent program of speech training. In one instance a bird had been receiving dedicated speech training for over a year. The bird, when I saw it, was still completely wild and had never made any sound other than that of a wild bird.

Although there is little, if any, scientific evidence to support it, parrot fanciers, amateur and professional alike, are virtually unanimous in their belief that if you and the bird are going to accomplish anything together, the bird must be tamed first.

Taming any wild creature carries with it the connotation for most of us that in the process of becoming tame the wild creature *loses* something of its natural self. I cannot address this for all wild creatures, but in the case of parrots, just the opposite is true. In the wild parrots have been observed to engage in playful activities, and while feeding they have allowed human observers to approach quite closely. In contrast, however, the caged, untamed parrot lives, it seems, in a state of anxiety. The process of taming a parrot, I suggest, takes nothing

Stick-training your pet bird is one of the best ways to begin the taming process. *Left:* Yellow-crowned Amazon. *Below:* Blue-fronted Amazon. *Opposite:* Lesser Sulphur-crested Cockatoo.

away from its nature but will in fact allow that nature to develop and permit its playful, friendly individuality to bloom. When it becomes accustomed to your presence and the direct physical contact of perching on your wrist, your parrot should lose its anxieties about being in human company. As it gains experience through repeated contact it will look forward to your visits. It is true that some birds don't enjoy and may object to a lot of handling, but very few birds once tamed want to be left completely alone. If you encounter a bird that won't perch on its owner's wrist willingly, the bird either hasn't been tamed or that particular bird and its owner have a compatability problem. Once the parrot and its owner have endured the taming process, the bird is going to feel a lot better and happier about its situation. It learns finally that these huge creatures outside its cage do not pose a threat but in fact can be counted on to provide a liberal supply of yummy food treats. The naturally friendly parrot will begin to focus on its human owner, and more than likely a good friendship will follow.

The experts all seem to agree, through the experiences of many individual pet owners, that the birds which develop the most extensive verbal repertoires are those which enjoy solid friendships with their owners. There are always the exceptions, of course; I don't doubt that there are many untamed birds that still talk. I would be surprised, however, to hear of an untamed bird with an *extensive* vocabulary.

When you take your bird home, make up your mind that you will tame it, regardless of how long it takes. If you find eventually that you cannot accomplish the task, go back to your pet dealer for advice.

There are many methods which are used successfully for taming parrots. Every expert trainer naturally thinks his or her own methods are the best but admit that there are few hard-and-fast rules. In this chapter I will describe the method that I used for taming Siegfried. It is a method used by a professional tamer of my acquaintance.

Before actually getting into methods, it is important to understand some of the basics which apply to the taming of any wild creature. Our cats and dogs need no taming even when very young because they are the products of thousands of years of domestication. Every puppy born of a pet dog is completely equipped with "inherited memories" of man as a friend and benefactor. His primal instincts are somewhat repressed because he no longer has any natural enemies, worries about food, or concerns about shelter.

Your new parrot, however, has a different background. It is extremely unlikely that it was born in captivity. Most likely it was captured in its native country while very young and then has changed hands a few times. It may have been caged in overcrowded conditions and held in quarantine before it finally arrived at the retail pet store. It has, from a human being's point of view, been treated well with regard for its physical health. I believe it safe to say that from the bird's point of view the experience has been a threat to its security. The next thing that happens to it at the pet store is a constant exposure to curious humans peering and poking. The pet store deals in other pets of course; the incessant yapping of puppies, the sounds of other birds, and (worst of all) the malevolent gaze of a boa constrictor all keep it a bit on edge.

Amazon parrots have a reputation for being very steady birds and easy to tame, but I think that before making an attempt to begin taming, the tamer must tune in to the bird's frame of mind. The bird you buy may not have had the traumatic experiences I have described above. The pet store owner will, I hope, be more profes-

This Jandaya Conure is being trained to step from its perch to the training stick.

Opposite:
Now that the conure steps from perch to stick, the trainer will have the bird practice this exercise until it steps onto the stick whenever it is presented.

Cockatiels are very popular as affectionate pets, and some are talented mimics. Most are easily tamed.

sional than to accommodate a bird within sight of a natural enemy. I would recommend that once you have selected your new pet, you start thinking about its experience from *its* viewpoint.

Your bird is still wild in spite of perhaps many months of captivity. Its instinctive concerns are for safety, food, and shelter from the elements. Its primary senses for staying alive are extremely keen eyesight and hearing, and its primary defense against danger is flight. Basic taming may be accomplished fairly quickly or it may take weeks. It depends entirely on the individuality of the bird and the skill of the trainer. In many wild-animal taming situations, the tamer accomplishes his mission by establishing dominance over the trainee. With parrots this is *absolutely* not the approach to take. Tameness is accomplished only by convincing the bird of your intentions to protect it from danger and remove its worries about food and shelter. If during taming you show fear of being bitten, anger, or any attempt to dominate the situation, you will not succeed. Now that we have some of the basics covered, we are ready to select the trainer. It really makes no difference to the bird whether you are a man or woman, but don't let a young child tame the bird. A man has tougher hands, generally, and is more likely to be able to deal with the pain of a hard bite. Men, though, have a tendency to be a bit too direct in their approach to the bird. Women tend to be considerably more gentle in approach, but their smaller, more delicate hands are likely to suffer. In deciding who will do the taming, keep in mind then that the tamer must have these qualities: lack of fear of being bitten, patience and perseverance, gentleness, and a bottle of Mercurochrome. Of course, only one person should do the taming.

Hand Taming

To begin, you should have a cardboard carton of pretty good size, about 16 × 24 × 16 inches deep. Cut the flaps off or push them down inside so that they are snugly against the walls. The carton will be used horizontally with the open side facing you. Other equipment you will need are two sticks (natural tree branches), about one inch in diameter and twelve inches in length, and a supply of sunflower seeds. If a woman is to be the tamer, she may prefer to wear gloves. They should be tight-fitting and skin-colored.

It is best to begin training as soon as you get the bird home, most experts agree. The bird will be a bit bewildered by the ride from the pet store, confined in a dark box (in Siegfried's case, a paper grocery sack). This temporary disorientation will aid you and your pet. Place the bird in the carton in some room of the house

Before moving onto the trainer's hand, this African Grey tests it with its beak.

Opposite:
The repetition of having a parrot step up from finger to finger accustoms the bird to perching on hands. *Above:* A young Plum-headed Parakeet. *Below:* A Yellow-naped Amazon.

where you won't be disturbed. Let the rest of the family leave the room and close the door. Your friend's wing should be clipped so it cannot fly. Seat yourself on the floor in front of the carton so it cannot escape, but don't crowd it. Very, very slowly take a few seeds and place them inside the carton.

Now reflect for a moment on the situation. You have a wild bird trapped, and you are going to convince it that you are its friend. This is the moment to put yourself inside its feathers and consider how it evaluates the situation. Escape is out of the question, so if it sees any sign of a threat to its safety, it can only stand and fight. Begin talking softly to it, and keep talking while the session is in progress. Give it plenty of time to look around and evaluate whether or not it is in danger. Make all of your movements very slowly—any sudden motion will trigger its defenses. Place one of the sticks on the floor inside the carton and give the bird plenty of time to examine it. Don't worry about time; let this first session last as long as it takes.

After exploring its surroundings by walking about a little, the bird may start to relax a bit. This will be indicated by its not standing quite so erect on its legs and by its neck being not totally stretched. If the bird eats a few seeds, this is a very good sign. It may walk to the stick and stand on it, another good sign. When you feel you and the bird are sufficiently relaxed, you can proceed to the next stage.

If it is already standing on your stick, you now attempt to pick up the stick with the bird on it. Otherwise, pick up the stick and slowly bring it across its body close to the floor. You want the bird to step on to it. Let the stick touch its legs, but don't press. Keep talking to it. If it doesn't step on or it runs away, back off and wait for it to calm down. When it does step up onto the stick, lift it just a few inches and stop again. Offer a few seeds

Using the technique described in the text, Growler (Grey Owl) steps onto the first stick and is brought clear of the box.

cupped in your free hand. Look on each little advance as an accomplishment, and don't try to rush your pet. Let the bird set the pace to some extent. Throughout the process, advance only when you see the bird is calm. Anytime it makes a growling sound, back off; you are triggering its stand-and-fight reflexes. If it moves to bite the hand that is holding the stick while it is perched on it, distract its attention with your free hand.

The next step is to produce the second stick and get the parrot to step from one stick to the other. Hold the second stick across your own body with the end resting on the arm which is holding the stick with the bird. Give the bird plenty of time to examine the stick before you slowly advance the stick toward it. If yours is a bird that gains confidence rapidly, you may find that it very soon wants to walk up your arm. Neither of you is quite

This young Cockatiel is taking its first cautious steps onto its owner's finger.

Opposite:
Outside the cage for the first time, the
Cockatiel is nervous.

The bird is now on the second stick held in the right hand and, gaining confidence, steps up again onto the first one.

ready for this, so use the free stick to block its progress. Let it step onto the free stick that you place in its path.

Once the bird is completely calm moving from stick to stick, and as soon as *you* feel ready, you can begin hand taming. Place the free stick on the floor and let it step onto your hand. Hold your hand on edge, fingers extended close together, thumb tucked into your palm. You may have observed that the bird tests each new perch with its open beak before it steps on. Don't panic when it does the same thing to your hand. If its beak starts to squeeze, say "No!" and roll your hand toward your body to disengage the beak. Be careful not to do this prematurely; remember the whole point of taming is to develop trust. You must trust the bird as you expect it to trust you. If you shy away as soon as you feel its beak, it will not consider you a reliable perch. Maybe the next time it reaches for your hand it will try to "catch" it before you pull it away. Once it readily steps onto your hand, dispense with the sticks as quickly as possible.

The next phase is to very slowly rise to your feet and move about the room. If the parrot jumps off your hand, give it a minute to calm down, then again offer it your hand to step onto. Don't chase it around the room.

If it at any time demonstrates fear and aggression, remember that it is behaving perfectly naturally under the circumstances. Get inside its feathers and ask yourself how you would behave. Don't at any point hesitate to back up to a previous phase of taming and repeat it. You should attempt to read how the bird feels by observing its body language:

The *aggressive attack posture* is demonstrated by the bird standing tall on his legs; the wings may be held slightly away from the body. The neck will be stretched full length and slightly arched, and the beak is open, pointing downward. All feathers will be pulled down flat, and the parrot will emit a growling sound.

The *alert wary posture* is similar to the above except that the neck is not arched, there is no growling, and the beak may be open or closed. During early taming the bird will exhibit these signs most of the time. When it begins stepping onto your hand, there is one more signal: the alert wary bird will grip your hand quite tightly, with claws dug in, so to speak.

Relaxed posture: if your taming efforts proceed smoothly, you will soon notice that your bird looks smaller and fatter. Its neck will retract, forcing the feathers to fluff; it will relax its legs to a squat on the perch, causing the body feathers to fluff. The beak will be closed, and the claws will be much looser on your hand.

The Cockatiel's initial reaction to being outside the cage for the first time is to take flight.

Opposite:
Above: After flying in panic around the room, the young Cockatiel lands on the branches of a bonsai tree. *Below:* Finding its first landing place unsteady, the bird flies off to land on a steadier perch, a shelf.

If you progress in the first session to the point of being able to move slowly about the room with the bird perched on your hand, you have made excellent progress. Put the parrot in its new cage with food and water and take a break. Let it relax for an hour or so, then have another short session. You can let the other members of the family in for a visit, one at a time. Instruct them on how to approach the bird, to make no sudden motions or loud noises.

Don't let the first session last too long, not more than an hour if the bird is not making good progress. If you are seeing a lot of aggressive posturing, the bird is under great stress and should be allowed to go to its cage. Let it relax for an hour; then start again. Ply the bird generously with seeds and small pieces of nuts after each taming session. Hand-taming is accomplished when the bird will step willingly onto your hand from wherever it is perched. Encourage other members of the family to make friends with the bird and to take it onto their hands. At this stage it should not yet be allowed to sit on anybody's shoulder. Some birds are inclined to do this and it is mistakenly read by owners as a sign of tameness. A bird that will stay on your hand is tamer than one that wants to move to your shoulder. Birds like to climb to high places, but your shoulder is one high place it isn't ready for.

When you have accomplished hand-taming, you will be able to handle the bird for routine cage maintenance. Obviously, tameness is a matter of degree. You may have observed that some birds are considerably more tame than others.

Using the method described here, Siegfried's first taming session went beautifully. Within about twenty minutes he was stepping confidently from one of my hands to the other. Another fifteen minutes after the initial hand-taming I could walk about the house with him, and he was also hand-tamed to the rest of the family. It was difficult to believe he was the same bird who just a short while earlier on the dealer's premises looked so vicious. As is usual with professional handlers of untamed birds, a heavy glove was worn to get Siegfried out of the cage. Even through the glove the dealer was able to feel the pain of several hard bites.

Biting

Some parrots are so gentle by nature that they will not even consider biting their owner unless severely provoked. However, if you buy a young untamed bird or an older bird which is not especially friendly to strangers, there is a very good chance that you are going to get bitten. The first thing you should know about getting bitten is that most bites are minor nips. Parrots do have incredible strength in their beaks. This strength is very rarely used on the owner, but it is still very common to get a "hard" bite, which may or may not break the skin, depending on how the bite is administered. If your bird grips your finger using the extreme point of the upper mandible and the front, cutting edge of the lower mandible, then with even moderate pressure it will probably break the skin. Most bites are not administered in this manner. The bird will usually hook the upper mandible over your finger and squeeze it with the lower mandible brought up from underneath. Most of the time you can disengage from the bite before it gets too hard, because the bird really doesn't move very fast.

When you get used to being around a bird that does bite, there is a tendency to be a little careless. The reason for this little paradox is that if you aren't afraid of being bitten in the first place and you become accustomed to the bites, the tendency is to ignore them. I am as guilty of this as many other parrot owners and handlers, but

Gaining confidence, the young Cockatiel starts to walk around and peck at things. Here it is nibbling on ornamental ivy.

Opposite:
Quickly becoming bored, it starts to peck at the furniture. If left unattended, a bird can do a lot of damage to household goods with its strong beak.

The trainer must judge when to dispense with the sticks and work with the bird on his hands. This decision is made mainly by the likelihood of being bitten. This particular bird turned out to be remarkably gentle, but its nervous nature made it a challenging subject for taming.

my recommendation is that you work with the bird to modify his behavior.

With young, untrained birds the main reason for biting is purely defensive. You have it trapped so that it cannot escape by flight, and you compound that by approaching to touch it. The bird sees this as a threat to its security, so it defends or attacks to defend. In this respect I consider fear and aggressive biting to be the same in that they are both born of insecurity.

Once you get your bird past basic taming, you may be tempted to feel that it isn't going to bite you anymore. This may well be the case, especially if you don't continue into advanced taming. In other words, if you don't press the bird's tolerance, you won't annoy it and it may see no need to bite.

Some birds insist that you play with them, and if you

enjoy playing with them, the game sometimes gets a bit rough and tumble. Parrots are noted for their flashy tempers, and with familiarity your hands, and especially your fingers, become its toys. Under these conditions I believe that many birds bite for fun in the same manner that they chew up their other toys for fun. Remember the last time you played with a kitten? The claws are extended all the time the kitten plays. With a grown cat the claws are retracted when it plays with you, but when the game really becomes fun, out come the claws. The cat doesn't *intend* to hurt. So it is with a parrot; its beak is its primary touch sensor.

It will be an ongoing part of your experience with the bird that you tell it a loud no when it bites. It is smart enough to learn how hard it can squeeze before you object. Let it know that you don't like to be squeezed very hard at all.

In the case of a very stubborn bird who won't listen to reason about biting, you may have no recourse other than some form of punishment. Let me say that only in cases of extreme biting should any form of punishment be used on a parrot. While the bird is being tamed and is still afraid, biting or attempting to bite is perfectly natural for it. *Never* punish the bird for *any* reason during taming or any other form of training. To repeat, punishment should be considered *only* for excessive biting. If you don't cure the biting problem, the bird could seriously injure you or some other member of the family.

If you absolutely have to punish the bird, then the first thing to do is to simply put it back in its cage. Everytime it bites you say "No!" loudly and let it know you don't want to play with it. After it has had a few minutes to reflect on its sins, let it out again. Give the bird plenty of time to connect biting with being put back in its cage before trying anything else.

To prevent further damage to the furniture, the Cockatiel is offered a piece of lettuce, but the bird is a little bit hesitant about approaching the hand holding the lettuce.

Opposite:
Above: Parrot-like birds respond to the human voice, and soothing words can quickly calm a nervous bird. *Below:* After its first trip into the world outside its cage, the Cockatiel now returns to it, waiting patiently to be let in. Daily supervised exercise is essential for the bird's health, and it will soon gain confidence in itself and in you.

If after a couple of weeks you have made no progress, you may have to be more direct. Immediately after getting bitten, speak a loud, angry no and flick your fingernail against the side of its beak. It is imperative that you do *not* do this repeatedly. Once is enough. The bird will understand this, even if it is too mule-headed to understand anything else, because it will be similar to the sensation of being pecked by another bird. Now·put the bird back in its cage and leave it there. Over a period of time the bird will expect to get "pecked" if it bites, so it should stop. If this isn't effective, see your bird dealer. He may know a professional who can help. If you ever find yourself getting angry because of several painful bites, take a deep breath and just put the bird back in its cage. *Never* try to work with the bird while you are angry.

Parrots and People

There are some behavioral characteristics which in my experience and opinion are mistakenly attributed to parrots. One of these is the rather frequent statement that a certain bird likes women and hates men, or vice versa. I consider this statement to be patently absurd. Parrots have difficulty determining gender even within their own species. As intelligent as they are, I doubt seriously that they have a grasp on the concept of gender in humans, let alone the ability to determine which is which.

I can believe that some birds as individuals might like or dislike deep voices, the smell of ladies' makeup, long hair or short hair, and many other sights, sounds, and smells of humans. The right combination of factors may lead to a bird liking or disliking most women it encounters—not because they are women, only because they are most likely to exhibit the characteristics which it likes or dislikes. Sound reasonable?

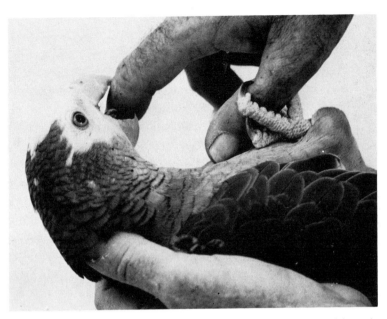

Acrobatic play like this often results in play bites which, although sometimes painful, rarely break the skin.

Some months ago I accidently proved this to myself in a pet shop which I was visiting for the first time. As I was looking about I saw a beautiful Lesser Sulphur-crested Cockatoo perched in an ornamental tree. I sauntered over for a closer look, stopped several feet away, and began talking to him. After a minute or two to let him get used to me and for me to size him up, I slowly continued my approach until I was within touching distance. Still talking to him I offered him my hand as a perch. He looked at the hand carefully, then tentatively stepped on. After a moment I brought my other hand up and began ruffling his face and neck feathers. He obviously enjoyed this handling, and we were instantly pals. After several minutes I reluctantly returned him to his tree to continue my shopping. When I reached the cash register, the lady said something like, "You sure seem to have a way with birds." I com-

An alert, steady gaze is a good indication of a bird's tameability. Don't bother buying a bird that displays frantic behavior as you approach its cage. Easily frightened birds are difficult to tame.

Opposite:
When your parrot engages in extensive preening while sitting on your hand or wrist, it is a sure sign that his tameness is advanced. Siegfried is very likely to permit handling as long as his preening isn't interrupted.

plimented the cockatoo as being a nice, gentle bird, and she said, "Yes, he is, but you're the first man who has ever been able to touch him." Of course I don't know why that particular bird was willing to make friends with me, but obviously I wasn't demonstrating the characteristics it had learned to dislike. (A word of caution: it is not a good idea to offer your hand to a strange bird, as a matter of habit, unless you have an unlimited number of extra fingers.)

Parrots will sometimes develop a fixation for their favorite trainers and forbid others to handle them in any way. This is another example of a behavior which, in my opinion, parrot owners have made too much of. It is quite reasonable to suppose that if one individual spends the time necessary to tame a particular bird, that bird may become tame only with that one person. To all other persons it may seem to be still untamed. The bird, from its own viewpoint, may not be forbidding other friendships but only insisting that others earn its trust and friendship in the same way as its first trainer has had to do.

Siegfried was originally hand-tamed to all members of our family, but during the following several days he withdrew his friendship from all but me. The other family members weren't too keen on sharing the many scratches from his claws and occasional bites which they saw me receiving, so they contented themselves with enjoying him from a discreet distance. This arrangement was quite mutual. Siegfried enjoyed having anybody sit near his cage and talk to him, but physical contact was forbidden. During this time he made it my responsibility to be sure other members of the family didn't get too close when he was out of his cage. Many times while Siegfried was sitting on my shoulder, if somebody else stepped up too close, he would squawk and give my ear a nip. As time went by he got to know the rest of the

It is very important that you spend the time necessary to tame your pet. If caged and left untamed, it is quite possible that a bird will not engage even in normal wild-bird play activities. Siegfried's appetite for fun stems entirely from the complete feeling of confidence and security which is acquired through taming.

family very well and, fortunately for my ears, became less demanding of protection.

Most fixations of this type should not be thought of as permanent or irreversible. Parrots are by nature friendly little creatures, and although a particular bird may always relate primarily to one person, most birds prefer many friendships.

It was not my intent that Siegfried become a one-person bird. His fixation on me was due simply to the fact that I was spending a great deal of time with him and had paid my dues to earn his trust. In our family Siegfried was generally regarded as dad's hobby. Only my wife and two of our three daughters felt, as animal lovers, the challenge of wanting to win his friendship. They each experienced the discouragement of being nipped a few times, and all but my wife Ellie gave up pretty early. She decided to win him over by leaving him in his cage and talking to him from a nearby chair. Progress has not been fast, but Siegfried and Ellie have now become very good friends. His conduct with her is not predictable; sometimes he will perch on her wrist and sometimes not. Ellie is not allowed any real intimacy by Siegfried yet. While he is on her wrist, she isn't allowed to touch him with the other hand.

Siegfried is, however, more fond of Ellie's voice than any other, and this factor is a sure promise of a close friendship. Ellie can teach Siegfried to speak a phrase usually in just a few minutes. Two of these phrases came as a result of simple games. She noticed that Siegfried would hang from the mesh of the cage, close to her, when she approached. One day she tickled his chest gently and said, "Gitchy-gitchy-goo." This simple act was an enormous success in building their friendship. Within a few minutes Siegfried had mastered the phrase and showed enjoyment with the tickling. Some weeks after this, noticing how his feet were extended while gripping the mesh, she extended a finger tip and tickled the sole of his foot, at the same time saying, "Tickle-tickle-tickle." This game was met with the same enthusiasm. Another phrase was added, and the friendship developed further.

I urge the reader through these examples to show patience and perseverence with your pet. Don't allow some of the myths and legends one hears from time to time to discourage you from experimentation. Keep in mind that your pet is not familiar with this old folklore and therefore is not likely to be influenced by it. I believe that if there is one magical thing you can do to develop a friendship, it is to offer considerate, gentle care—and even then it may take a long time.

A playful bird will regard anything it can grasp with claw or beak as a toy. Jewelry, shirt buttons, watch bands, and pens may be damaged.

Advanced Taming

As you and your pet play together everyday and begin speech training, you will be building on your relationship of trust. Over a period of many months your bird will most likely become increasingly tame. This author has developed some guidelines to enable you to envision how tameness might typically progress. Use it as a guide, but remember that each parrot is a unique individual.

TAMENESS SCALE

1 — The parrot will step from its cage to your hand, from one hand to the other, from your hand to its stand or cage, and will remain on your hand or the stand without jumping or flying off.

2 — Allows you to touch its beak and rub its feet; remains seated on your hand or wrist while you walk about.

3 — Allows you to touch its chest and facial feathers; will preen its feathers while seated on your hand; will play with a toy or eat a snack while seated on your hand; will walk up your arm and sit on your shoulder while you walk about; will preen your hair and ears.

4 — Allows you to ruffle facial feathers, stroke the top of its head and neck. Hangs upside down from your fingers; sits on your shoulder and snuggles up to your face or will take a little catnap; will sit on your hand and exercise its wings.

5 — Allows you to ruffle feathers on back of neck, scratch its neck, stroke its back, cup your hand around its back, grasp its tail feathers; hangs upside down from one hand and allows your other hand to support its back; allows you to gently swing it back and forth while it hangs from your hand by one or both feet; hangs from your fingers and beats its wings; performs other hand-to-hand acrobatics; allows you to hold it in both hands like a pigeon.

6 — Allows you to touch its body under wings; will nestle down in your hands; will lie on its side or on its back, while its head may hang down looking about or be curled up preening leg feathers—will probably be holding your finger with one foot.

7 — Allows you to spread its wing partway and ruffle its body feathers at base of tail, tummy, and legs; will nestle down in your cupped hands and catnap; allows toenails to be clipped and filed while sitting on perch.

8 — Allows you to fully extend one wing to inspect feathers; allows you to probe and examine new feather growth while body feathers are fluffed up.

9 — Allows you to fully extend both wings; will lie on its back in your cupped hands without holding onto you with its feet; will also lie in this position on your lap while you trim and file its toenails.

10 — Allows you to touch it any way you want to without protest; allows you to clip its wing feathers while lying on your knee or seated on its stand.

The author would like to emphasize that this guide is not intended as a *blueprint* for increasing tameness. It is intended only as an *illustration* of how tameness may progress. Each bird is an individual and will progress differently.

Many birds don't like to be overly handled, but some others learn to enjoy it. Handling by its owner is something each bird has to learn for itself. In order to make progress with advanced taming you must be just as patient, gentle, and understanding as you were during hand-taming. It takes a lot of time for the bird to get used to all the new sensations. At various times during advanced taming it will make objections to what you are doing. Be considerate, back off, don't press. It has a life expectancy of over fifty years, so there's no hurry.

Siegfried is typical of Amazons in his fondness for playing, with toys in his cage and with his trainer. I have used this playfulness as an opportunity to develop his

This Orange-fronted Conure is quite tame and accepts having its head petted.

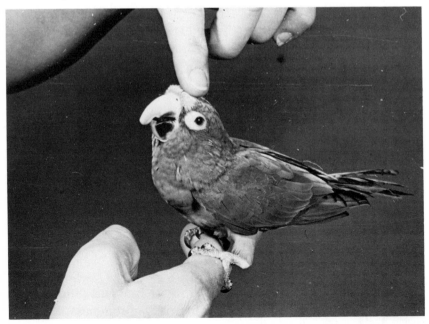

Feeding your bird by hand also helps to develop tameness.

tameness. It is a simple matter to devise little games which will get him used to being tickled on the back of the neck, scratched on the back, etc. Each advance you make in touching him increases his tolerance to touch and, accordingly, his tameness. One of the best opportunities I have found is when the bird is perched on your hand preening itself. The bird becomes so engrossed in caring for its feathers that it doesn't notice your hand touch it. This may not work the first time you try it, and you may get nipped a few times. Keep working on tameness during all your activities with the bird. This is very much in the bird's interest as well as your own, because with increased tameness comes confidence and a feeling of security about its new home.

I devised the Tameness Scale because although many feel that taming is accomplished when the bird is basically hand-tamed ("1" on the scale), I take the more conservative view that taming is accomplished when the

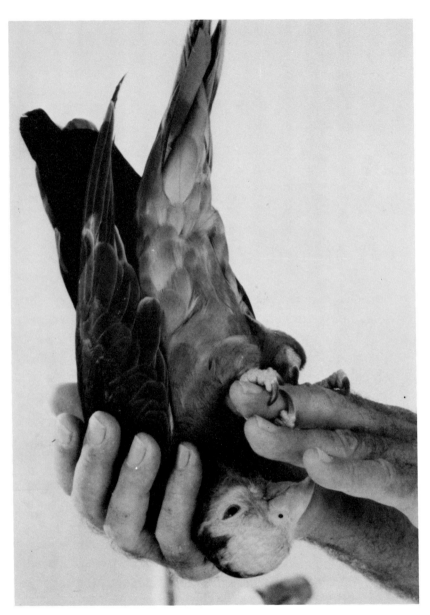

Amazons are known for their highly individualized personalities and variable moods. When Siegfried wants to play with his trainer, almost any form of handling is permitted. He shows his most excited, playful mood by raising his head feathers and rapidly dilating and contracting his pupils.

trainee loses interest in eating the trainer.

Siegfried's advanced taming is of course an extension of basic taming. Using the Tameness Scale as a point of reference he now would rate about a "7." Advanced taming is an ongoing process which will last as long as you and the bird are together. Siegfried is still convinced that this is another game: if I can tickle him, he can give me a bite. He bites not in objection to the tickle, it seems, but to show his interest in the game.

In the section on biting I made reference to parrots biting for fun. Siegfried is a good example of this trait in that he seems to enjoy the kind of rough-housing normally associated with puppies. In parrot terms Siegfried is in his childhood, and compared with young animals I have known, his behavior is very much childlike. Sometimes while playing with a toy in his cage, if it doesn't do what he wants—say, come apart fast enough—he flies into a rage and attacks it savagely. In some of our early sessions I used to play with him while he was in the cage with one of his toys. Experience has taught me to let him play his "war games" alone. He plays too rough for me.

Our usual play sessions now are conducted out of the cage. When he comes out of the cage, we exchange a system of greetings consisting of words and whistles, to which he adds a few clucks. He usually walks up and down my arms, across my shoulders, and steals the pen out of my pocket. A lot of hand-to-hand acrobatics follow, with Siegfried swinging himself into one-claw-grip upsidedown positions with almost suicidal abandon. I believe this carelessness is part of his childlike frame of mind. During play sessions of this type, where the bird may get more and more carried away by the heat of battle, I find it very easy and, may I add, very necessary to change the mood. Parrots can change their moods very rapidly, going from great docility to anger and back again in less time than it takes to write the

Sitting on your shoulder, your pet may become very curious about any shiny objects and begin to view your jewelry as its toys.

words. When play begins to get too rough, I find the mood can be changed by some simple action on my part. If I stand up, walk to a window, or begin talking to one of the family, the old game ends. You might find this useful when your own parrot becomes too rambunctious.

Siegfried enjoys being swung about while hanging from my fingers, so every play session includes some of this. Exercise great care when you let your pet perform some of these stunts, because although the legs and feet are incredibly strong, he musn't be allowed to overstrain muscles and tendons. Don't attempt to force any kind of play on the bird; it isn't necessary. Let it "tell" you what it wants to do. As you and your pet get to know each other, you will learn how to read it.

Sometimes Siegfried doesn't want to play at all. At these times he is quite content to climb to my shoulder and snuggle against my ear, or sit on my hand and settle

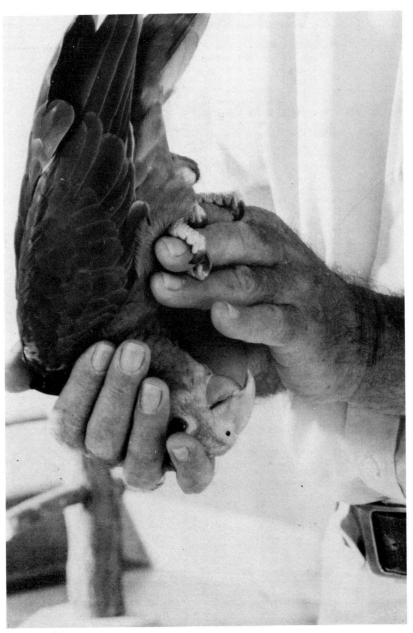

Preliminary to one of Siegfried's favorite games: hanging from the author's hand while being swung about.

to a sleeping position. Your bird will enjoy just being close to you at times, so be flexible.

Case History:
A Tough Little Bird Named Growler
Throughout this volume I have stressed that parrots are highly individualistic. As a consequence of this fact the reader will gather that training and taming efforts will not necessarily produce predictable results. I believe it conceivable that you might encounter a bird of such a high-strung and frantic nature that would make it, for all practical purposes, untamable. Likewise, some individuals of a species known for its talking abilities may never say a word.

What follows is a description of an unusual situation involving an African Grey Parrot and a very nice young couple I will call Bob and Mary.

Background information: Bob is a professional artist with considerable experience in training birds. He has little background with parrots but spent some years as an amateur falconer. He has tamed and trained many hunting hawks and other birds of prey. Mary is also a professional artist and has had considerable success in taming their pet Cockatiel. "Peaches" can whistle a couple of tunes, speaks a few phrases, and responds with affection to all the attention bestowed by Bob and Mary.

Bob decided to buy a parrot for Mary as a birthday present. Due to its reputation as a nice pet and a good talker, he decided on an African Grey.

The particular bird that he bought had been in stock at a local pet store for several months and was known to the employees as Growler. The bird apparently was already high-strung (not uncommon among Greys) and had been subjected to some teasing by young visitors to the store. At the time I met the bird he had been Bob and Mary's pet for about eight months. They had made many attempts at various times to feed fresh foods and a variety of dry foods; but Growler, at times very angrily, threw everything out of his cage except his passion: sunflower seeds. Eventually they became resigned to allowing him to eat only sunflower seeds.

His behavior wasn't any better than his eating habits. He would perch for brief periods on Mary's wrist or shoulder but wouldn't have anything to do with Bob. When Bob approached his cage, he would fluff his feathers and cry in the rather nerve-wracking manner of African Greys. Mary did not escape this disrespectful treatment either. Sometimes, when standing close to the cage, Mary would observe him lean toward her and with his neck fully extended click his beak at her. Mary had spent time hand-taming Growler. Having reached a point where she felt that was as good as he was going to get, she began speech training. The bird did not respond to this. In fact, while his owners were in the same room, he would make no sound at all. He was such an introvert that not only was he silent in the presence of people, he wouldn't even eat while anybody was in the room with him.

My involvement in the situation came about through the casual discovery that Bob and Mary and I shared a common interest in birds. I was somewhat incredulous at their description of Growler's behavior, knowing the African Grey's excellent reputation as a pet. We arranged for me to meet him, and it was suggested that maybe I would like to "have a go" at him. Growler was everything that they described; he started howling as soon as we were within a few feet. This loud howling or growling was the one sound he *would* make when humans were present. I didn't really need another bird to play with; Siegfried already consumed a lot of my spare time. Growler's behavior, however, was a challenge I couldn't resist, so we agreed that he would come and stay with me for a week.

Upon getting him home and settled I decided that the first order of business was to use the information I had been given and my own first observations to analyze the problem. After that was done I could determine a course of corrective action.

The problems: (1) Growler is not eating a proper diet. Sunflower seeds are supposed to contain a mild narcotic. If this is true, the bird could be in a state of narcosis. In a phone call my favorite vet, Dr. Fitzpatrick, suggested that the bird may well have become psychotic. This is not uncommon, and it would probably take about thirty days to detoxify the bird's system by feeding a correct diet. (2) Growler won't eat in the presence of his owners or play or make normal parrot sounds other than crying his objections to human presence. (3) Although he will perch on Marys' wrist or shoulder, he doesn't usually do so willingly. He doesn't enjoy this human contact and shows fear or hostility to Bob.

Physical condition and effects of poor diet: The bird is considerably underweight; eyes are clear, but pupil is almost constantly contracted; body temperature and respiration appear all right. The leg scales give the appearance of a young bird, and by rough deduction he should be at least two years of age. The plumage of head, neck, torso, and legs is complete though rather dull looking. All flight feathers indicate serious nutritional problems. He had, as accurately as I could count, only five or six tail feathers (about half the normal complement). On his right wing I could count only three primaries (out of a normal ten), and on his left wing he had only four or five. I could not count secondaries without manhandling him, which I decided was not advisable at this time. The flight feathers that he did have, including all coverts which I could see, were dull and lifeless in appearance. His primaries in particular were very tattered. Quite obviously he was molting, as the loss of feathers indicated. The truly surprising aspect of this was his inability to fly. If he were in his natural habitat, he would die. Without the essential ability to fly, he wouldn't be able to hunt food or escape danger. Apparently, through refusing proper foods, he had trained his owners to discontinue offering them. Now he was discarding old feathers but didn't have the nutrients in his system to grow new ones. Growing new feathers places additional physical stress on a healthy bird, so it follows that an undernourished bird will be under even greater strain. In summary, Growler, through his refusal to eat properly and his antisocial behavior, had deteriorated into a physiological and psychological basket case.

The solutions: The most immediate necessity was to get the bird onto a proper diet. I reasoned that there was little hope of correcting behavioral problems while his physical health was in such poor condition. His new diet was going to follow what I recommend for Amazons and accordingly would include all fruit I could get him to eat, plus a variety of other dry foods. I was determined that under no circumstances, except the most extreme, would he get any more than two *measured* tablespoons of sunflower seeds each day. The reader will recognize that the seriousness of the problem required drastic measures.

I brought Growler (now renamed Grey Owl by his owners, to help give him a new outlook) to my home in his own cage. We located him in the corner of one of the bedrooms for the first night. The corner position of a room, away from walk-by traffic is the best location for a nervous bird. With Grey Owl's (I will use his new name from now on) cage in place, I removed his sunflower seed and replaced it with a mix of chicken scratch (cracked corn, oats, and a variety of other small seeds) and some peanut kernels. Next I provided another dish of chopped fruit chunks and gave him fresh water well dosed with vitamins. His fresh food was fortified with Super Preen in powder form and brewer's yeast.

This done, I left him to his own devices for a couple of hours and realized that this particular case was an excellent opportunity to further my experience with birds. I decided to keep a detailed log of all events, treatments, and results for future reference. When I returned to see how he was doing, he greeted my arrival with his loud crying. I talked to him softly. As I slowly approached his cage, I was happy to hear the crying diminish to a dry throat-rattle sound or low growl and see his extremely ruffled feathers flatten to almost normal.

He had been exploring his food supply; food chunks were spread around the cage. I couldn't determine if any seed had been eaten, but some peanuts had. I picked up the fruit chunks and returned them to his dish to let him know that bad table manners were frowned upon. I got the cage tidied up, accompanied by a lot of growling. I then took a chunk of apple and held it to his beak. He evaded the apple every way he could, and each time that he took it and spit it out, I picked it up and held it to his beak again. A parrot will automatically touch its tongue to anything it picks up in the beak until it knows what it is holding. Obviously, I gambled that if the tongue touched the apple often enough, it would recognize it as a food item and, even if an unfamiliar food, would acquire a taste for it. I finally got him to nibble off some small fragments of the apple and swallow them. On this first day I also spent about twenty minutes working on hand-taming. As stated earlier I didn't expect to make any changes in his behavior at this point, but I felt it

With a very nervous bird, a lot of repetition is advisable. Here, Grey Owl is again being drilled in stick training.

very important that he know something about his trainer. He had been able to tame his owners into feeding him sunflower seeds and not handling him very much. He had to learn that he wasn't going to be able to train me to allow these bad habits.

The following day I decided that many of his bad habits might remain fixed so long as he was in the security of his own cage. In other words, if he had a territorial fixation on his cage, he might be more resistant to new ideas. I moved Grey Owl to a spare cage and placed him in the family room where he would be in constant contact with the family. Grey Owl's one night of solitude in the bedroom was as close as he got to being molly-coddled.

There are, I believe, very few absolutes to cling to in these situations. The rightness or wrongness of a course

145

of action is more reliably determined by the results it produces rather than by whether or not it follows the rules. During the next three days Grey Owl received a lot of attention about his eating habits and tameness behavior, and considerable progress was made: (1) He no longer growled loudly at me; he growled loudly at other family members only if they approached too quickly. (2) Would now eat in the presence of people but would stop if anybody but me got really close. (3) Would eat sunflower seeds out of my hand (this was mainly because the only way I would allow him to enjoy his passion was as a reward for good tameness performance). (4) Developed another passion, for peanut kernels, which he now got from my hand for superior training performance.

He was still on a ration, and would remain so, of sunflower seeds. Peanut kernels were now also rationed to ten kernels a day. In fresh-fruit consumption (which now included apples and pears) he was eating about one-fifth of the volume I would consider normal.

At the end of our first week together Grey Owl had made further progress: (1) Would eat considerable quantities of fresh fruit, which now included apple, pear, orange, grapes, and nectarine, although most of the time this had to be hand-fed one chunk at a time. Was also eating the chicken feed, dry cat food, and walnuts enthusiastically. (2) Would now eat without hesitation, even with people around. (3) Had ceased his loud crying completely and would only low-growl and ruffle his feathers when surprised. He didn't greet me with any kind of growling and would only occasionally ruffle his feathers slightly. (4) In taming would step willingly to my hand, although he still wasn't calm enough to want to stay. Would allow me to touch his feet, legs, chest, and neck and under his wings, without any protest. The taming sessions during this period were conducted many times throughout the day and were of about five minutes duration. (5) Would occasionally make some chirrup and whistling sounds. (6) Developed a fascination about my fingers and during feeding would try to bring himself to explore my fingers with his beak. He did nuzzle my fingers several times but only with great shyness. Wouldn't let me touch his beak.

At the end of this first week I gave Bob and Mary a progress report. They came over to visit and said they could see noticeable improvement in his behavior. I asked if I could keep him for another week just to cement some of the changes. They agreed to this, though I could almost hear Grey Owl thinking: "Please take me home. This guy is a slave driver."

The week that followed showed more improvements. The bird was eating well, and his disposition and tolerance of humans vastly improved. He no longer cried or showed any antagonism to anybody but would still low-growl and ruffle his feathers if approached too quickly. He now made normal parrot sounds in the presence of humans, and he frequently used a foot to eat his food.

As of this writing Grey Owl, back at his own home, is continuing his progress toward becoming a healthy and happy bird. I hope the pet parrot which you choose will not make the demands upon you that Grey Owl had made upon his owners. If you do happen to encounter a difficult bird, I hope you will view it as a challenge to your imagination.

Siegfried demonstrates that when hand taming is accomplished the parrot should sit calmly on his trainer's hand and make no attempt to fly off. Once tamed, the bird can start to receive speech training.

Speech Training

The parrot's ability to imitate human speech is unquestionably the most persuasive factor which makes these birds so popular as pets. Why they imitate speech and other sounds in captivity is at present an unsolved mystery. Quite logically it is widely believed that in the wild state they maybe use this talent as part of the social or mating ritual. But there is currently no scientific evidence to show that in the wild a parrot makes any sound other than the sound of a parrot. There is *some* evidence that parrots do not mimic other birds. Therefore, why such a remarkable talent? We can only guess and be grateful that the talent is there. I am going to assume that you have some hopes of teaching your bird to talk. With this assumption in mind I will acquaint you with some methods which I have found very successful. This will require the coverage of some fairly basic knowledge. Teaching the bird starts with teaching the teacher. There are no iron-clad rules when it comes to training parrots, so I would like you to keep your own creative imagination in high gear and ready to make adjustments as you see the need.

The first thing I would like you to do is to take a small piece of notepaper or an index card and make a sign to stick somewhere on your friend's cage. Place it where he can't chew it up, but where you will see it whenever you approach the cage. The sign should read, in big block letters, Be Patient, He's Only A Little Bird. Go ahead and do that now. I'll wait for you.

Before we expect too much of the parrot, we should

reflect on the mechanics of human speech and our normal use of our own abilities. We produce our speech sounds by expelling air from the lungs. The outrush of air is articulated by the vocal chords, throat muscles, tongue, palate, teeth, and lips. The parrot's vocal apparatus is very different from ours, so it has its limitations. Most particularly the parrot has no lips, so it cannot produce the slight explosive sounds that we make when we say the word *pepper*. We won't go through all of these limitations; they are far less important than the sounds that it *can* make. Be aware, however, as you select its vocabulary, that its strengths in imitating your speech lie in those sounds which we produce in the throat and middle mouth. Its limitations are in the frontal mouth sounds. Some owners on reading these statements might say, "Well, my bird can say, 'Polly wants a cracker.' " They are quite right if they maintain that is what they *hear*. What the bird is actually *saying* is more like *golly gants a gracker*. Siegfried says a very convincing "Oh boy"—at least that's what we hear. By listening intently we realize he is actually saying *oh goy*.

The next very important aspect of speech I would like to deal with is our everyday use of the language. Our easy familiarity with speech and communications with other humans causes us to be more than a little careless. We seem determined to eliminate from our speech every sound which isn't absolutely essential to conveying the message. This will work for human communications, but if the parrot learns this style of speech, chances are we won't understand what it is saying. There are three important factors to keep in mind when you begin your training sessions on a particular word or phrase:

Articulation: This is the actual production of all the sounds of a word. I would suggest writing the word you're teaching on a piece of paper before the training session. Pronounce the word aloud several times; have

The sign states the main point to remember in speech training.

another member of the family pronounce it. If you have a tape recorder, by all means use it for practice.

Pace: The common image of the talking parrot involves short, clipped phrases, barely understandable because they are spoken so rapidly. Ask yourself if you've ever heard of a parrot who could say "Hi, y'all" in the slow drawl of a Southerner. It just doesn't fit the image, does it? This is the fault of the trainer, not the bird. I would suggest speaking very slowly during your training sessions. If you use as a point of reference the slow Southern pace of speech, I think you'll be happy with the result. Your bird will not necessarily sound like it is speaking too slowly. When it couples the careful articulation with the slow pace, its speech will have a very deliberate quality.

Inflection: Language instructors prefer the word *intonation,* but *inflection* is more commonly used to describe the expression we place on various word sounds to convey subtleties of meaning. Without inflection our speech would sound flat and mechanical, rather like computer-simulated speech. When you select a word to teach your parrot, decide on the inflection you want to use and be sure to use the same inflection every time. Remember, he's only a little bird. If you change your inflection from one session to the other, and especially if you alter the articulation and pace, the bird may think it's a completely different word. This kind of variation on the part of the trainer could result in a dismal failure for you and the parrot. Practice out of your bird's hearing and consider the word you have selected in terms of articulation, pace, and inflection.

There is no question that the voice quality of a woman or child is easier for a parrot to imitate than the deeper, gravelly voice of a man. If you are a man and are planning to train your bird, don't be discouraged by this fact. My normal voice is about average in pitch and

152

When you are teaching a bird to imitate human speech, it is very important to enunciate your words carefully.

a bit gravelly, but I have been able to overcome this drawback in training Siegfried. In our own family our daughter Dawn has the combination of voice quality, patience, and dedication to be a good trainer for Siegfried. On the other hand, her schoolwork didn't permit enough time during the early phase of his training. My voice has the poorest quality, but I had the time and other necessary qualities. I overcame my voice problem by simply practicing the training words at a higher pitch.

The sounds of the human voice can be compared to those of a piano; the voice of a child might be said to be in the high middle range, while a man's voice is at the low end of the keyboard. A parrot's voice is very wide in range, but his most "human" sounds fall within the high middle range. Please keep in mind that we are talking about Amazons. I have found that if I raise the pitch of my voice just high enough to eliminate the gravelly tones and achieve a musical quality, Siegfried can imitate it.

For his first training sessions I followed as closely as possible all of the advice I had been able to find in the books I read. I took Siegfried out to a quiet room in the house which I use for an office and began training him on the word *hello*. In order to describe inflection for the rest of this section I will use capital letters to indicate a high-pitched sound and small letters to indicate lower sounds. This is important to some explanations we will be offering as we progress. Using these devices, the inflection on the word *hello* in these first sessions was *HEllo*. After the first few sessions Dawn and I recorded a tape of the same word. On the thirty-minute tape, Dawn recorded fifteen minutes and I did the other half, meticulously abiding by what I have mentioned about articulation, pace, and inflection.

The early sessions, as I mentioned, were conducted in my office, away from the distractions of household sounds. During these sessions, always thirty minutes in duration, Siegfried seemed to be easily distracted by little sounds: the barking of a distant dog, an aircraft high overhead.

As time went by and as I continued to observe his behavior during training, I concluded that an environment with too much silence, in Siegfried's case, is not necessarily a good thing: it seems to suppress his inclination to make sounds. This made me wonder how often and under what circumstances it gets deadly quiet in the jungle. Do sensible parrots keep quiet when the predators are hungry? Do the carelessly garrulous birds get eaten first? Siegfried's behavior in this respect has modified since that time, due probably to learning that under his present circumstances silence is not a danger

Gail Murphy, training Siegfried to say, "Ahoy, matey," is amused when he insists on replying, "Hi there, how are you?"

signal. If the reader has a young bird exhibiting this kind of behavior, you might consider leaving a radio playing for your friend if you are away at work during the day. It doesn't have to be loud, just enough sound to break the silence.

During this early period we began use the tape to supplement my instruction. The usual routine was to play the tape for him at about 7:00 AM each morning. The tape player was placed right next to his cage. Following this I would train him personally for thirty minutes in my office from 8:30 to 9:00 AM. At various times throughout the day I conducted a number of minisessions of about five-minutes at random intervals as my work permitted. (I have already described play-and-taming sessions that Siegfried and I have together, so the reader will know this isn't all work and no play.)

Siegfried made his first attempt at the word *hello* after six weeks of training. Let me inject here that during the six-week period the training routine was followed without any appreciable variation. The need for consistency on the part of the trainer is stressed by all writers on this subject. Well, Siegfried's first *hello* came as something of a surprise and taught me a most important lesson. His inflection on the word wasn't at all the inflection we had been teaching him. It was so different in fact that the other family members were as mystified as myself about where he might have heard somebody say *hello* in this particular fashion. His inflection was HELL*lloo*OO. His pronounciation, starting high, going low, then ending on a rising inflection sounding remarkably like a doting grandparent speaking to an infant child. Over the next several days, with me now training him on the new inflection, his word attained a beautiful clarity and of course was full of expression. It was very amusing to all of us to be spoken to as children by this wise-looking little bird. In the process of helping him with the new inflection we discovered who the guilty party was: it was myself. Apparently, when I approached his cage at various times, I would unconsciously use an inflection commonly used when addressing a baby. The point here is that as his first word Siegfried learned a sound that was considerably different from the sound he was taught. To us humans the two sounds are still the same word, but to the parrot one was considerably more *interesting*—so much more interesting, in fact, that he ignored the sound he heard many, many thousands of times in favor of a sound he heard maybe a couple of hundred times. I haven't forgotten this lesson, and in all subsequent training I make a point of using inflection that is interesting to the bird.

The time element of six weeks may be typical; I don't

know. Writers indicate that if one thing is certain, it is that this depends on the individual bird and his trainer. The first word might come in a week or two, or some months. It is this uncertainty which is the most trying for the trainer. After several weeks have gone by without a response, the trainer begins to wonder if the bird will ever talk. During these times of frustration the best advice I can offer is that you go visit your parrot and read the sign on its cage.

Once the hurdle of the first word is passed, additional words come easier. During the two-week period which followed Siegfried's first word, he acquired ten additional words, could meow like a cat, laugh, and produce several human-type whistles.

Some trainers use food rewards for any kind of response to the training word. I believe this is a good idea if you do it consistently. My attempts to follow this method were not successful. First of all, Siegfried didn't make any of the parrot sounds which are supposed to precede words. During the out-of-cage training sessions I had plenty of treats to give him but couldn't reward him for anything until the end of the session. I rewarded him then for showing up for class. Later on, when he was saying his first word and was in his cage, rewarding was physically cumbersome. I had to open the cage and pass the treat up to him, sometimes dropping it. By the time he got the reward he most likely didn't know why. So instead of a food reward I use a spoken compliment, and this has worked very well. Whenever he gives the response, during a lesson or at any other time when I talk to him, I say a very enthusiastic "very good!" He likes this so much that he now uses it himself.

Many trainers value the tape recorder highly as a training aid. You avoid much of the boring repetition of saying the same word or phrase over and over. I still recommend that you add your own live voice to the

The tape recorder is useful for training the trainer as well as the parrot. You can listen to the many different ways a phrase can be said before choosing which one to teach your pet.

training so that the tape only supplements your own training efforts. Siegfried isn't too keen on the tape method of training, so his response is usually to take a little nap. Occasionally I have heard him produce a low, growling sound that mimics the sound of the motor of the tape player. He also seems to enjoy imitating the sound of the tape being rewound.

During the early part of Siegfried's speech training, before he spoke his first word, he would attempt to imitate almost anything *except* the human voice. He could do a good imitation of the clothes dryer and even produced little clucking sounds as buttons on the clothes struck the drum of the dryer. If your parrot is engaging in this type of extracurricular activity, look on it as a positive sign. The bird *is* imitating, so it has the *desire* to imitate. The bird will eventually begin to imitate you because your presence and companionship will become more interesting to it than the other elements in its environment.

One of Siegfried's phrases came about almost by accident. Noticing that he liked to "shadowbox" (that is, pose his head in one position, then begin darting it about as if chasing a fly), I devised a game to play with him, like the peekaboo that one might play with a child. My main objective in this was to increase his tameness, and if he actually learned the phrase, so much the better. When his head stopped darting about, I would suddenly say "Peekaboo" slowly and deliberately, in a high- pitched voice. It only took two ten-minute sessions for him to learn the game, including speaking the phrase. It is still his favorite game. He has difficulty saying *peek*, and his closest rendition has been *gekadoo*. If you think about it for a minute and pronounce the word, you will realize that the word is almost entirely a frontal mouth sound. We tend to forget these limitations even when we know about them.

I would recommend having each day one main training session of at least thirty minutes' duration. Also the session should be early in the morning, at approximately the same time every day. As your time permits, you can add shorter sessions to reinforce the main session.

The main session is best conducted out of the cage, preferably with the bird on your hand or wrist. With the bird on your hand you have a better chance to keep its attention from wandering. Another reason for this is that the physical contact between you and the bird builds the relationship.

If your bird begins preening while you are training, don't let it bother you too much. I believe preening is an itch-induced reflex, and when it has to scratch, it has to scratch. When Siegfried gets really engrossed in preening I make a guess about whether he is still listening. If

The author and Siegfried engaged in speech training.

his head disappears under a wing and is gone for a while, I usually tap him on the shoulder and tell him to pay attention. Parrots are intelligent enough to attempt to distract your attention from the lesson if they just aren't in the mood for it. For this reason I suggest that you plan the content of each lesson before you begin. Don't let the parrot lead you away from the plan, or it will be training you. Let me elaborate on this. After your parrot gets past its first few words, with continued good, solid training its vocabulary may increase very rapidly. Your training sessions will then require a constant review of all its current words and phrases, plus training on the new phrase. While the new word is being spoken by you, the trainee may use every trick it knows to distract you. Other pet owners will agree with me when I say that a well-spoken parrot has an irresistable charm and knows how to use it. I must confess that Siegfried has led me astray more times than I care to admit.

For your short sessions too, have a particular plan in mind. I always conduct these wherever Siegfried happens to be: in his cage, on the stand, or while playing with him. An ideal time for a minisession is while you are feeding your bird or tidying up its cage.

In selecting his first words it is important to count the syllables of the word. Start with a two-syllable word and, I would suggest, stay with two-syllables until the bird has learned several words. The first few words allow your parrot to succeed and to enjoy the pattern of success. I don't really consider what the bird learns to say very important. The important thing is that it develops a habit of learning new sounds. (Almost all writers state that in their opinion parrots that talk are happier birds.) If you concentrate on the simple sounds first, the bird will be allowed to develop its vocal abilities along verbal lines. Some simple words are

During training sessions, parrot pupils are likely to become restless and mischievous. This Blue-front is preening its handler's hair.

Opposite:
Siegfried decides to preen
and scratch a while.

these: *hello, hi there, bye-bye, oh boy, thank you, chow time.* When you think he is ready, go on to some three-syllable words or phrases, such as *how are you?* As his repertoire continues to grow, you can begin coupling words and phrases, such as *hello, how are you?*

Shortly after you begin speech training, make a list of the simple phrases which you regularly use near your pet. These might be such things as: *How are you today? Are you hungry? What a pretty bird! Is that good?* These phrases should be spoken just as clearly and slowly as you would if you were actually training. Place an interesting inflection on the phrase so that you almost sing it, and use the phrases in a consistent fashion. If you key your phrases to specific activities, your parrot will learn the association and will most probably pick up the phrase. On the day that you arrive at his cage and your pet greets you with "Oh boy! Chow time," you will consider this additional effort well worth it.

Parrots have a high level of intelligence, as already mentioned, but they do not use a *reasoning* ability in the use of human language. They do have a rather incredible knack of saying just the right thing at times. I have mentioned that I use the spoken compliment "very good" to reward Siegfried during training. As I say it, the inflection is a very exaggerated *VERry GOod.* Siegfried eventually picked it up and would pronounce it very clearly in the same exaggerated way. One day my daughter approached his cage and said a coupled phrase he was just learning. In response to each "Hi there, how are you," he replied, "Very good," as if complimenting her on her pronunciation.

Parrots are also credited with very human behavior at times. I saw an example of this when he was learning *thank you.* I approached his cage, looked up to where he was sitting on a high perch, and said, "Siegfried, thank you." He immediately replied, *"Thank aBoo."*

When I laughed aloud, he seemed to become annoyed and scolded me severely in parrot language, shrugged his wings, and strode back and forth along his perch. I had the uncanny feeling that his parrot-language tirade would translate into human language as "Be patient, I'm only a little bird."

The reader may wonder, "If parrots are such good mimics, why does it take so long to learn the first word?" We can only speculate. A major factor on the bird may be that it needs a certain amount of time to build a personal attachment to his trainer. Developing an interest in the sound of the human voice would certainly be another factor. The bird won't imitate anything unless he is interested and curious about the sound. Observations of Siegfried have demonstrated repeatedly that when he is most curious about household sounds such as those made by a food blender or a dishwasher, he will attempt an immediate imitation.

An additional possibility is that the human voice may be a challenge to its mimicing abilities. Once the bird makes an attempt to imitate you, its voice quality will usually improve rapidly. Sometimes you may notice that a particular word doesn't come out too well, but the bird will keep working to improve it.

I read somewhere, or once heard somebody say, that "teaching a parrot to whistle is about like teaching a fish to swim." If that was intended to mean that it is easy, I agree. I don't agree that it is pointless.

Some time ago I was talking with my son about a jungle film which had been shown on television. In the course of the conversation I mentioned to him that although the location of the story was the jungle of Burma, the soundtrack included the calls of two birds native only to Australia. Hollywood filmmakers had long ago decided that the calls of the kookaburra and the riflebird sounded so like "jungle birds" that they

Any location at home can be used for speech training, but in this case the unfamiliar outdoor setting provides many distractions.

Opposite:
The tape recorder can be a very useful
tool for training all kinds of parrots.
Siegfried, however, insists that his training be "live" but enjoys listening to
taped music for entertainment.

have been a part of almost every soundtrack ever since. The sounds are usually used one immediately following the other, something like *ku-ku-ku-ku-ku-ku-ku-ku-ka-ka-ka-ka-ka* (the kookaburra) *arouwww arouwww* (the riflebird). Listen for the sounds the next time you see a jungle scene. The point of the story is that during the conversation Siegfried was sitting on my wrist enjoying a play session. My son didn't remember the bird calls from the film and asked what they sounded like. I wasn't too keen on attempting the imitation, but he talked me into it. Siegfried's reaction was immediate. He emitted a few *ku-ku-ku*s then looked at me with a how-does-the-rest-of-it-go? expression. It took a week or so of "private" training sessions before he could do it well. During this period my own rendition became much better, so we learned together. Siegfried's kookaburra-riflebird imitation amuses everybody who hears it, especially since he sounds so like a human doing a bird.

Siegfried has also learned some human-type whistles. He finds it entertaining and so do I. The fact that he can learn these so easily reinforces his habit of learning, and our communications have another dimension. As an example of this I taught him the "wolf whistle." This is his favorite, and he enjoys experimenting to produce different versions. When I'm working away from his cage in the adjoining room and can't talk to him, we will sometimes whistle back and forth to each other. The game has advanced to the point where I whistle just one note and he provides the other. Or he whistles both notes at a high pitch; I whistle back at a lower pitch, and he repeats lower still. I use this as a further example of your pet's versatility of mimicry and, as an aside, note that the human whistling as Siegfried does it bears little resemblance to the natural sound of a bird.

If you feel inclined to teach your bird any human

whistles, I would recommend strongly that you wait until after its first few words. Don't teach it to whistle as a substitute for speech. Teaching your parrot to imitate a variety of nonspeech sounds is not necessary, but many birds learn such sounds very easily, and they can be amusing.

The parrot's wild call is a harshly unpleasant sound; heard once is enough. If your training can provide it with enough vocal exercise, it may feel less need to go native. There will undoubtedly be times when your pet will want your attention and, if you are out of the room, will "call" you. This is a time when it is likely to use an extremely loud natural call. Siegfried still lets us all hear this call once in a while, but through a series of events, we have learned how to reduce it.

One of our six cats is named Spot because of her unusual dog-like markings. When she was a kitten, in the manner of kittens, she would seek tiny nooks in secluded places to sleep. When it was mealtime for the cats, some member or members of the family would have to search room by room, calling Spot. Needless to say, Siegfried eventually picked it up and would add his voice to the mealtime search. For some reason best known to himself Siegfried identified the name Spot with me. It became very amusing to my children to hear him call "Spot! Spot!" sometimes when I would leave the room. We also noticed that "Spot" replaced the wild call which he had been using. Naturally, I couldn't let him continue thinking I was "Spot", especially since he also developed the impudent habit of preceding the word by a whistle commonly used for calling a dog. Teaching him to call my name involved sitting about twenty feet away from him. Over a period of a few days Siegfried learned the name Kev, which he pronounces *KE-eh*. He uses it when he wants me to come and talk to him, but he isn't completely convinced that *KE-eh* is my

Sometimes Siegfried is coaxed into a talking mood by a combination of spoken words and whistles.

Opposite:
An occasional bite is to be expected even between friends. Notice that Siegfried has hooked the upper mandible over the thumb so that the extreme point is not employed.

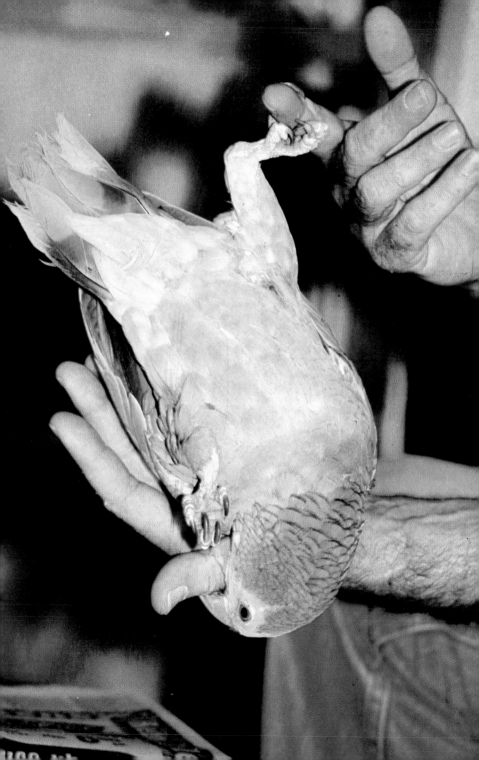

Cato and Spot, two of the author's cats, watch Siegfried as he climbs about in his cage.

name. If I don't respond after a couple of *KE-eh*s then he calls me by my *real* name which, of course, is "Spot."

Do work on this aspect of your pet's training. After he has acquired his first few words, teach him to call your name. If you can eliminate his wild screech, both you and perhaps your neighbors will breathe a sigh of relief.

So far we have been talking about *imitative* speech, where the bird simply repeats what you have said. A far more complex pattern of training is required for *responsive* speech. An example of responsive speech is asking the bird a question such as "Hi there, how are you?" and it replies, "Very well, thank you." For responsive speech you generally start off by first teaching the bird to say the answer to the question. Then you can couple the question to the answer by saying the whole thing.

When it recognizes the general sound of the question, it will remember the part it knows and will say it with you. Don't let him get to know the question too well or the bird will begin using it. The trick is that when you feel it recognizes the question, you stop and let the bird finish it by providing the answer.

In one instance with Siegfried I used a much simpler technique which worked very well. I wanted to be able while he was eating to ask him, "Siegfried, is that good?" and have him reply with an enthusiastic "MMM-mmm!" In the training session I would say "MMM-mmm" twice, ask the question "Is that good?" then say "MMM-mmm" once more. "MMM-mmm" was always spoken just a little louder and with considerably more inflection (the inflection is identical to that of the wolf whistle). He learned it just the way I had hoped and in addition will also say "MMM-mmm" sometimes when he is eating without hearing the question. This latter illustrates the parrot's ability to associate words and phrases with activity.

The reader has probably encountered the term *command speech* applied to the training of parrots. This means that the bird has been trained to speak the appropriate word or phrase at any time the trainer wishes it to. With performing birds in shows this kind of performance and training is a necessary part of the act. Not all birds are sufficiently willing or talented to perform in this manner. Professional trainers select their potential stars very carefully and then, of course, apply their professional skills to the process.

Your own training efforts may produce a very eloquent bird, but don't be surprised if it doesn't always say what you want it to say when it is supposed to. Siegfried is a very talented little fellow with a pronounced individuality. He enjoys the attention of the family but has a stubborn streak a mile wide. I have

Naturally, a bird enjoys flying most of all, but apparently Siegfried was captured in the wild before he learned to fly; and shortly after capture, he had his wings clipped. Observing him teach himself to maneuver in the air when his new flight feathers grew provided the author with one of the many rich experiences which come from the study of these fascinating birds. Siegfried has been trained to fly, on command, to the hand or shoulder.

Opposite:
Many birds enjoy having the backs of their heads scratched and will bend the neck and fluff their feathers to invite a scratch.

Siegfried and the author have developed a very friendly relationship.

discovered that one does not command Siegfried to do anything. We are allowed to *suggest* that he perform a particular trick or speak a phrase; then he decides whether or not it is a good idea. This situation has produced much more entertainment and amusement than if he simply repeated what he heard. Now that he has acquired a fairly extensive vocabulary, Siegfried attempts to employ it much as we humans do. Very commonly we engage in amusing, nonsensical little conversations which typically go as follows:

Siegfried: "Hi there!"
Trainer: "Hello."
Siegfried: "How are you?"
Trainer: "How's my little bird?"
Siegfried: "Very good. Is that good? MMM-mmm!"

Another:

Trainer: "Ahoy, matey!"
Siegfried: "Ahoy, little bird."
Trainer: "How's my little bird?"
Siegfried: "Ahoy, Siegfried. Poor little bird. Ahhh."
Trainer: "Is that good?"
Siegfried: "Ha! Ha! Ha! Tickle-tickle-tickle!"
Trainer: "Cato." (Cato is one of our cats.)
Siegfried: "Cato. Here, kitty-kitty-kitty."
Trainer: "Very good, Siegfried. Very Good."
Siegfried: "Very good. MMM-mmm."

The reader will surmise quite accurately that some of the phrases used here by Siegfried were picked up accidentally or, even more interestingly, were assembled by himself from other known words and phrases. This illustrates that a bird which enjoys using human speech sounds develops an intuitive sense, if not a reasoning ability, about how they are used.

During my studies of parrots I have encountered numerous stories attesting to the marvelous degree of vocal development they can achieve. The author of one story impressed me particularly with the statement that one of his birds had converted its communications entirely to human language. All of its moods, he said, were expressed in words. It is interesting to read of such an experience, but watching Siegfried's gradual assimilation of human language and hearing some parrot sounds made with a "human" voice is incredibly fascinating.

In many instances Siegfried has shown an ability spontaneously to assemble a physical act, a spoken phrase, and a display of mood or emotion in a very human fashion. Let me give an example: One day during the summer it was an unusually warm, 105° outside, and inside the house it didn't feel much cooler. I had

This well-cared-for Cockatiel is providing its trainer with an "instant replay" of her words and whistles.

Opposite:
Siegfried will happily sit on the author's shoulder and play with a toy or even fall asleep.

179

just finished a project I was working on and went to visit Siegfried. He was sitting on his upper perch and panting from the heat. I said, "Oh! Poor Siegfried. How are you feeling?" He opened and closed his beak a couple of times and replied with a long, drawn-out "Oh boy." I decided he might feel more comfortable if I gave him a bath; at least it would cool him temporarily. Shortly after feeling the coolness of the spray his normal perky spirits returned. As he got wetter and wetter, he became more and more talkative, and I was treated to his entire repertoire of phrases, whistles, and sounds. We talked, whistled, and clucked to each other while I dried him with the hair dryer. With his bath complete Siegfried, obviously in high spirits, walked up my arm to my shoulder, gave my ear a playful nip, and said, "Tickle-tickle-tickle." Then, jumping up and down with excitement, he laughed hysterically.

On another occasion one of my daughters was watching a television program but was being distracted by Siegfried's boisterous chattering. Finally, exasperated she said, "Siegfried, be quiet." As she tells it, he immediately looked dejected and said, "Poor Siegfried. Ohhh! Poor little bird. Aaah!"

Siegfried still uses a lot of what I can only describe as parrot language. These sounds, however, bear little resemblance to the sounds of an untrained bird of the same species. It is quite possible that a bird may become so accustomed to mimicking the human voice that it prefers those sounds to its own language. On the few occasions when Siegfried has met other parrots he has never used his "native language." On one occasion we had a friend's parrot as a house guest for a couple of weeks. I was naturally interested in knowing how Siegfried would react to the visitor. When the new bird's cage was settled in place near Siegfried's, I took

Siegfried out of his cage so they could meet. Siegfried eyed the stranger, then very politely said, "Hello, how are you?" Needless to say, this caused great amusement to all present except the untrained visitor. I placed Siegfried on top of the visitor's cage, and he walked headfirst down the cage, looked in, and said, "Peekaboo."

The visitor was fairly quiet during his stay because of the unfamiliar surroundings, but when he did squawk, the sound was so alien to me that I had to remind myself that this was the natural sound of an untrained bird. Siegfried must have considered the sound to be pretty alien also because he showed no interest in it.

The reader may be reaching the conclusion that the development of a bird's vocabulary is a sort of haphazard process. To some extent this is true, because once your bird acquires its first few words, it has discovered a whole new world of entertainment and communication. It becomes an active participant in the selection of words and phrases. As it begins to make a sound resembling one of your commonly used phrases, you will naturally begin to help by drilling the bird on it. The only caution I would suggest here is that you don't neglect your own training plan and don't try to train it on too many phrases at the same time. If you keep up the training, you will undoubtedly reach a point with your bird where it knows a couple of dozen phrases, you are training it on your current phrase, and it is working on maybe two or three phrases that it is just picking up. To order priorities I would suggest training mainly on your phrase. In your shorter sessions drill it on one of its own phrases, the one which it is saying best. Lastly, for any other phrases the bird is picking up, just use them more frequently around his cage. The key here is flexibility. Don't be reluctant to change your training plans

The full coloration and complexity of the flight feathers can be appreciated from this view of the Double Yellow-headed Amazon in flight. Notice that a few of Siegfried's feathers are not yet fully grown.

Opposite:
Among parrots the African Grey is "the man in the gray flannel suit." Note the pale gray scalloping on the feather edges and the lighter gray breast and belly. Many parrot fanciers prefer the coloration of birds such as Grey Owl to that of the gaudy Amazons.

Ellie Murphy and
Kelly exchange a few
words.

to meet the interests of your pet. Once it has learned
your phrases, you may want to devote all the training
time to *its* phrases.

Let's summarize our various points about speech
training:

> For all your training sessions choose the time
> which is most convenient, the environment
> most free of distractions, and have your bird
> out of the cage.
>
> Select your training words with the bird's
> limitations in mind.
>
> Remember to *articulate* precisely, speak at a
> very slow *pace* and employ interesting *inflec-
> tion.*
>
> Speak within a pitch range that your bird can
> imitate.

Be consistent in your training sessions as to time of day and length of session. Have sessions *every day.*

Use tapes only to *supplement* the trainer.

Reward your bird for attending class and compliment or reward it for progress.

Keep an open mind about what the bird wants to learn, and don't be preoccupied with teaching an organized vocabulary.

Invent games which encourage it to pick up a word or phrase.

Keep its early training simple and let it enjoy the pattern of success.

Review its current vocabulary every day so that it doesn't drop any phrases.

Use a few simple phrases consistently when near its cage.

Teach it some other sounds *after* he has learned a few words, especially a substitute for the wild call.

Be patient, it's only a little bird.

Your parrot will most probably reward your patience handsomely. Keep in mind that if you are going to be together for a long time, there's no hurry.

When selecting your first parrot look for some of the features
Siegfried displays: well-formed beak with a well-fitting lower mandible; clear, steady eyes; round, clear nostrils; and full, healthy
plumage.

Opposite:
Siegfried exemplifies the eminent
tameability of certain species of parrots
and the strong bond of companionship
possible between pet parrot and owner.

At the time photographs were taken for this book, Siegfried was about sixteen months old.

Index